VISUAL QUICKSTART GUIDE

PAINT SHOP PRO 5

FOR WINDOWS

Ben Sawyer
Joann Meyer

 Peachpit Press

Visual QuickStart Guide
Paint Shop Pro 5 for Windows
Ben Sawyer and Joann Meyer

Peachpit Press
1249 Eighth Street
Berkeley, CA 94710
510 524-2178
800 283-9444
510 524-2221 (fax)

Find us on the World Wide Web at:
http://www.peachpit.com

Peachpit Press is a division of Addison Wesley Longman

Copyright © 1998 by Digitalmill, Inc.

Editor: Corbin Collins
Copyeditor: Joli Kornzweig Bennett
Production Coordinators: Amy Changar and Lisa Brazieal
Compositor: Owen Wolfson
Index: Marie Nuchols

Notice of rights

Notice of Liability

ISBN 0-201-35362-8

9 8 7 6 5 4

Printed and bound in the United States of America

Dedication

To my parents for always being there for me
and to Michael for being my sounding
board and loving me anyway.

— Joann Meyer

To Dave Greely, the co-founder of Digitalmill
who has stuck through just about everything
to help make our company work.

— Ben Sawyer

Acknowledgments

Ben Sawyer:

After many books, I want to simply acknowledge my family and friends in general who've helped me through this and all the past work.

I'd like to especially acknowledge the staff at Peachpit Press. Having completed two texts with them, I can honestly say that their dedication to both authors and readers is truly a rare thing. I'm especially happy to know Nancy Davis, who had to leave us early on to give birth to her first child—congratulations! I also give a big thanks to Corbin Collins, who taught among many things that W can be a vowel. I am glad to be able to call him our editor and our friend. Thanks also to Nancy Aldrich-Ruenzel for her support to give us another authoring opportunity so closely on the heels of our previous work. And to Amy Changar, Owen Wolfson, and Lisa Brazieal for their patience and steadfast dedication to quality—this book looks as good as it does because of them.

I also want to thank Dave and Sherry Rogelberg at Studio B, our literary agents who keep helping us find the kinds of interesting projects and companies we like to work with.

Jasc, the creators of Paint Shop Pro 5, should be thanked for making such a great product. I've always been a fan of the little software company that could, and Jasc is such a company. Paint Shop Pro has become a great success.

Finally, let me thank Amed Khan, a good friend, who once again has failed to make the cut to dedication status—I promise next time.

Joann Meyer:

I have lived in Maine a little over a year, moving here from New York. I have a lot of wonderful family and friends back in New York and some new friends here in Maine who have helped make the transition a little easier. I would like to thank them all for their help.

I would like to thank my sister, Maryann, for always helping me and transferring to me some of her English skills. My brother, Louis, for encouraging me to make the move to Maine. And my brother-in-law and sister-in-law, Craig and Wendi, for making my brother and sister so happy and being so good to me.

My friends, Heather, Amanda, and Kassia, deserve to be thanked for always putting up with me and for being there for me through thick and thin.

I would like to thank the Flynn family, my future in-laws, for welcoming me into their family with open arms and to the Greens, Cappillinos, and the Hagues for their support.

Lastly I would like to thank my bosses, Ben and Dave, who hate that word, for giving me the chance to write this book and helping me along the way.

TABLE OF CONTENTS

TABLE OF CONTENTS

INTRODUCING PAINT SHOP PRO

Paint Shop Pro is a versatile, inexpensive software package that allows you to use your creativity and imagination to perform high-level image processing. This chapter covers the basic features of Paint Shop Pro and shows some of the ways it can help you realize your artistic vision. You also will learn how to organize and structure a Paint Shop Pro project.

About Paint Shop Pro

Paint Shop Pro is a well-known and widely downloaded image editing and processing package for Windows 95/98/NT. The product is now in version 5.0 (**Figure 1.1**) and offers much of the functionality of Adobe Photoshop 4.0 for a fraction of the cost. Also included in version 5.0 is Animation Shop, a great addition to Paint Shop Pro that allows users to quickly and easily create animated imagery for their Web sites, presentations, or other needs.

Is Paint Shop Pro the best image editor around? Well, Photoshop, Fractal Design Painter, and other products offer many advanced features and filters not found in Paint Shop Pro. But those products are more expensive and have higher-end requirements.

Paint Shop Pro is an excellent product for incidental users of graphics and imaging programs. Make no mistake, it is a powerful and capable program. But since it is available in shareware form, Paint Shop Pro is a bit less robust than other products. However, it is easier to learn and to use. Paint Shop Pro is the perfect choice for users who, although not graphics professionals, still need to create sharp-looking graphics.

Paint Shop Pro can also be used as a quick image conversion program for various graphics formats and for quick edits, such as cropping or lightening an image. Because the program loads quickly and requires relatively low CPU muscle, many professionals use it alongside other image editing programs for doing quick work on an image.

There are many great uses for this program. We'll highlight as many of those as possible throughout this book.

Simply sitting down and using Paint Shop Pro is a great way to spend a rainy afternoon, but

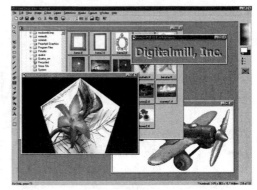

Figure 1.1 Paint Shop Pro 5.0 in action.

it is no way to get work done. Before you begin any project in Paint Shop Pro, you should have a plan.

We call this plan the *Paint Shop Pro Process*. It is nothing more than understanding the key steps and options that get you from start to finish with most Paint Shop Pro projects.

The Paint Shop Pro Process involves eight simple steps.

To use the Paint Shop Pro Process:

1. Acquire imagery.

   Using a variety of available options, produce the initial imagery from which you intend to build a project.

2. Get the color correct.

   Although you will constantly make color corrections throughout a project's life, it is smart to get the bulk of your color scheme and adjustments done early. Many filters and other effects are affected by the color of each pixel. By establishing the color levels early in the project, you will improve the results of filter operations later on.

3. Get the orientation settled.

   Set the orientation of an image with regard to size, rotation, and shape.

4. Apply filters.

   Many projects result from the variety of filters through which you can process an image. Whether it is to sharpen or blur an image, or to emboss it or coat it in hot wax, applying filters is a key part of creating an image's final form.

5. Apply deformations and effects.

   You can apply a number of effects and deformations to an image in Paint Shop Pro. The results of these features can be used to create quick drop shadows, 3-D buttons, and other shapes.

THE PAINT SHOP PRO PROCESS

6. Clean up the image by hand.

Although this is a step you may repeat throughout the process of creating an image, it will always pay big dividends. Once you are sure that you are done, check the image closely and fix any small problem areas.

You may find small scratches or dust generated by a scan, lens flare from a digital camera, or blemishes on someone's skin. Filters can create small, pixel-sized mistakes that stand out. Removing these imperfections requires a human touch that makes all the difference.

7. Save/Convert.

When you're completely finished with an image, you will want to save it. Paint Shop Pro supports more than a dozen image formats. Each one has its own features, of which you can take advantage.

8. Use the imagery.

What good is anything you make if you don't do something with it upon completion? In the case of Paint Shop Pro imagery, that usually means publishing it on the Web, using it in some other program, or producing a good printout.

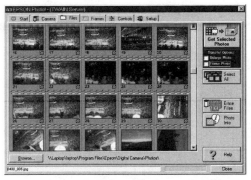

Figure 1.2 Most digital camera software easily lets you select photos from the camera and transfer them directly into Paint Shop Pro 5.0.

Acquiring Imagery

The first part of any Paint Shop Pro project is usually acquiring imagery to work with. Although there are many instances in which you might create something from scratch (such as creating buttons for a Web site), you will usually manipulate some image you've obtained from outside the program.

There are many different means of acquiring imagery worth considering. In Chapter 3, we cover each of these in more depth.

Scanning

Scanners allow you to convert any pre-existing picture, drawing, or other piece of flat work into a digital form. Scanners are excellent for converting traditional photos or a printed logo into a form in which it can be manipulated by Paint Shop Pro. Paint Shop Pro 5.0 supports any TWAIN-compliant scanner, so you don't have to leave the program to input scanned imagery.

Digital cameras

Digital cameras continue to grow in popularity. One advantage of using a digital camera is that any photo you take can be captured in a graphic form for Paint Shop Pro. Although cameras don't offer the resolution of scanners, they are usually much more portable. As a rule of thumb, if you need the highest possible resolution, use a scanned photo. When 640 x 480 or 1024 x 768 resolution will work, a digital camera is a great way to acquire imagery. Paint Shop Pro supports any TWAIN driver compliant camera software (as shown in **Figure 1.2**) and includes built-in support for two of Kodak's most popular digital cameras.

Clip art

Another way to acquire imagery for Paint Shop Pro is to purchase or download clip art.

ACQUIRING IMAGERY

There are two primary types of clip art available: professional clip art (which costs money) and freeware clip art (that you can download from the Internet and use for free). Before using clip art, you must be sure you have the rights to do so. When you purchase clip art, you are usually free to use it as you wish (although you can't resell it as is). When it comes to clip art that you find on the Web, though, be careful. Don't assume that it is free for your use. Check carefully to see if there is a license agreement or other information that describes what rights you have to use the artwork. Free Web clip art often can't be used for commercial purposes. Before using any Web clip art, be sure you understand completely the conditions for its use.

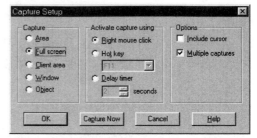

Figure 1.3 Paint Shop Pro is great for screen shot capture and processing.

Screen shots

Screen shots can provide you with another rich source of imagery (as shown in **Figure 1.3**). You may need to publish an image of a program running on your computer, or want to show a shot of a Web site. Paint Shop Pro 5.0 has some specific tools to help you in taking screen shots. It is one of the best programs available for quickly cropping, enhancing, and managing screen shots.

Figure 1.4 Adjusting colors such as the amount of red, green, or blue in an image is a snap with Paint Shop Pro's color tools.

Figure 1.4b Paint Shop Pro also includes tools to manipulate the structure of your image's palette, making color reductions and optimization of imagery for the Web easy.

Working with Images

Once you have opened an image in Paint Shop Pro, you can work on it with an amazing array of tools. As described earlier in this chapter, there are many possibilities for what you can do with Paint Shop Pro. Let's look at these in a little more detail.

Color changes

Color changes are a big part of working with any image, and Paint Shop Pro offers many tools to help.

Typical reasons to apply color changes including lightening an image, fixing redness in photos, converting an image to grayscale, or creating a negative version.

With nearly a dozen color effects, Paint Shop Pro is a great way to lighten an image, improve contrast, or reduce palette size.

The main functions to manipulate color fall into three categories:

Lights and darks: Many of the color functions, such as the Brightness/Contrast adjuster, affect an image's color scheme by changing how light or dark each pixel is. The lighter a pixel, the more color is pushed toward white. The darker, the more toward black.

Colors: While some color adjustments change only the lightness or darkness of a pixel's color, others (like Negative, Hue, and Colorize) can be used to change the base color of each pixel. By changing the colors of certain pixels, you can create entirely new looks (See **Figure 1.4**).

Palette structure: You can also change the physical structure of the color palette itself. This can involve lowering the number of colors in the palette (e.g., from 16 million colors to 256 colors) or increasing it (See **Figure 1.4b**).

Changing the palette is important because some effects (such as many filters) cannot be run on images with palettes that have fewer than 16 million colors. In that case, you can increase the palette, run the filters, and then decrease the palette.

There are times when you may want to decrease the palette size for other reasons; for example, you might want to decrease the number of colors in an image to facilitate quick downloads from your Web site.

Filters, effects, and deformations

Raw imagery is often not exactly what you want. It could be out of focus or too sharp. It may have too much noise in it, or you may want to add some noise (like the example in **Figure 1.5**) to make it look more old-fashioned.

You can run any number of filters that will help sharpen, blur, or add noise to an image.

Although filters merely manipulate an image's pixels, effects and deformations allow you to add items to the image or to physically warp it into other shapes or appearances. In **Figure 1.6** we used a cutout effect to add some highlighting around the edges of the car from **Figure 1.5**. Then in **Figure 1.7** we wrapped the entire image into a circle using the built-in Circle deformation tool.

All of these items are applied in much the same fashion. Select a complete image or an area on which you will run the process. After you set any necessary parameters, the process will change the image as desired.

There is also a custom filter tool included with Paint Shop Pro that allows you to create your own manipulations. Paint Shop Pro also supports traditional Photoshop filter packages such as Kai's Powertools or Alien Skin Software's Eye Candy.

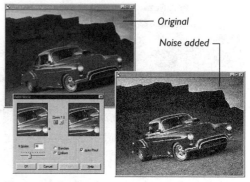

Figure 1.5 One of the strongest features of any image processing package is the ability to instantly change the look of an image through the use of filters like Paint Shop Pro's Add Noise filter.

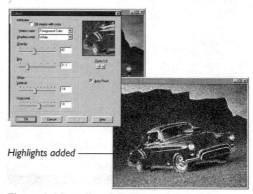

Figure 1.6 Paint Shop Pro's Cutout Effects dialog makes it easy to add highlights to imagery.

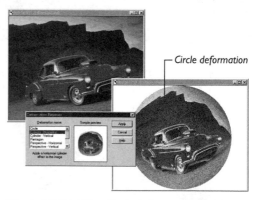

Figure 1.7 Paint Shop Pro includes ten deformations you can perform on an image.

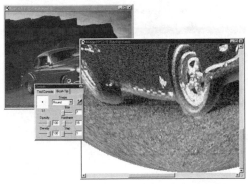

Figure1.8 Zooming tools, coupled with freehand painting, can help you add small details or touch ups to your imagery.

Figure 1.9 Resizing scans or photos for thumbnail display on the Web while maintaining optimal image quality is an easy process with Paint Shop Pro.

Painting and hand cleanup

To work with an image by hand you have many tools from which to choose. Paint Shop Pro features many brush tools for painting, including straight color drawing, a cloning brush that lets you paint over one section of a painting with that of another, and a retouching brush that lets you apply many of Paint Shop Pro's filter effects on a pixel-by-pixel basis. There are also basic tools for lines, rectangles, ovals, and circles, to name a few.

You can use these tools in two basic ways. You can create original artwork or you can further embellish an image on which you are working. For example, in **Figure 1.8** we zoomed in under a car's tire to add some additional shadowing.

Resize and crop

The size of an image often needs to be reduced (for use on the Web as a thumbnail) or cropped (so only the most important elements remain). These actions are easily handled in Paint Shop Pro.

Paint Shop Pro offers a cropping tool to do just that. The Resize feature allows you to increase or decrease the size of an image without destroying its appearance. In **Figure 1.9**, we resized the hot rod circle image into a much smaller version.

WORKING WITH IMAGES

Plenty more features

There are dozens more features that expand on the simple image manipulation features introduced here. As you can see, there is a lot you can do with Paint Shop Pro, and it is all fairly straightforward.

The trick to mastering Paint Shop Pro is to learn how to use each feature to its fullest potential. As with most graphics programs, there are lots of little tricks you can learn about each tool. Knowing them makes the difference between just using and mastering the product.

So after you've mastered the basics and played with the tools mentioned in this chapter, check out the detailed tips and techniques throughout this book that will improve your ability to use them.

WORKING WITH IMAGES

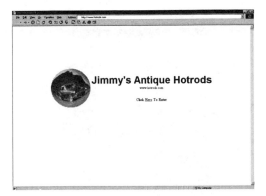

Figure 1.10 Thousands of Web designers count on Paint Shop Pro to help them design backgrounds, buttons, logos, and more for their Web sites.

Using Images

After you create and save a piece of work in Paint Shop Pro, you will probably want to do something with your creation.

There are really two ways to utilize the imagery you create in Paint Shop Pro. You can either print it out or display it electronically.

When it comes to printing your imagery, you can either output it to your local color laser printer or you can send it to a professional service bureau. A service bureau can print it at a much higher resolution, in larger sizes, and on heavier paper than you would normally have available at home or work.

Another option is to print an image onto thermal transfer paper and then iron the result onto a shirt or other piece of material. In fact, Hanes sells printing kits to help you accomplish this.

In terms of electronic output, you can insert your imagery into an application document, such as a word processing file or a Powerpoint presentation.

One of the most popular uses is, of course, creating graphics for a Web site. For example, the hot rod image we made could be a part of a simple logo greeting visitors to a Web site (**Figure 1.10**). We recognize that this is a major use of Paint Shop Pro and have included two chapters on creating Web imagery.

Paint Shop Pro 5.0 includes many special tools to help you create images and publish them on the Web. It has good support for the major Web graphics formats (GIF, JPEG, and PNG) as well as tools for optimizing the size and palettes of Web imagery.

What Else?

What else can you do with Paint Shop Pro?

Opening an image

People often obtain imagery over the Internet in a form that is not viewable by their Web browser. PSP is a good place to open that file because it supports so many file formats. You can view many images at a time with the thumbnail browser (see **Figure 1.11**).

Saving and converting

A major use of Paint Shop Pro 5.0 is loading images in one format and saving them in a different format. Only JPEG, GIF, and sometimes PNG imagery can be displayed by popular Web browsers.

Paint Shop Pro can convert images to these formats easily and even includes a Batch Mode (**Figure 1.12**) process to quickly convert more than 100 images.

Creating animations

Packaged with Paint Shop Pro 5.0 is Animation Shop (**Figure 1.13**). Animation Shop is a new application that lets you package individual frames of animation to create animated sequences that you can use to spice up your Web page or other presentations.

Figure 1.11 A built-in thumbnail browser makes it easy to sift through all the images you store on your hard drive.

Figure 1.12 With a batch conversion system built in, you can convert entire directories of images over to JPG or GIF for output onto the Web with the click of a button.

Figure 1.13 Animation Shop comes with Paint Shop Pro 5.0 and makes it easy to create GIF animations for your Web site.

Figure 1.14 You are not alone! Paint Shop Pro's history as a shareware title distributed online has made it one of the most popular programs ever. Over 50,000 people download it each week from C|NET alone!

Versatile + Powerful + Affordable = Usable

If we had to say one thing about Paint Shop Pro, it would be that it is a very *usable* package. There are many graphics packages but none that matches the easy access, versatility, power, and affordability of Paint Shop Pro 5.0. It's no wonder the product has been downloaded as often as it has and why thousands of registered owners use it daily. In fact C|NET's Download.com Web site named it one of the top ten most popular downloads ever in its history!

Now that we have a good idea of why we love it so much, let's dive in and learn how to get the most out of it!

SETTING PREFERENCES AND STARTING UP

2

As with any program, the basics of getting started can often be the most intimidating part of learning how to use it. In this chapter we cover a number of things that show you how to setup, configure, and get up and running with Paint Shop Pro 5.

Setting Up Paint Shop Pro

Paint Shop Pro has gained a majority of its popularity not just because it's a great program but because it is shareware. For years various versions of Paint Shop Pro have been available for free evaluation download on a variety of Web sites. Now it's shrink-wrapped too.

With the latest version you can download the shareware copy directly from JASC (**www.jasc.com**) and purchase it directly from them as well – right on the Web.

To install Paint Shop Pro:

1. Run the setup.exe program you down-loaded or from the CD by double-clicking on it in Windows Explorer or My Computer.

2. Follow the instructions and prompts, which are fairly standard for installing a Windows program. You're asked for a directory, and a few quick questions and in minutes the program is ready to run.

SETTING UP PAINT SHOP PRO

Figure 2.1 The Paint Shop Pro startup screen.

The Paint Shop Pro Screen

When you first run Paint Shop Pro you're greeted by the startup screen (**Figure 2.1**), which tells you the current status of the software (i.e. whether it's shareware or registered). Click Start to get past this screen and begin using the program.

The main Paint Shop Pro screen contains seven key elements:

The palette toolbar
The palette toolbar lets you quickly select foreground and background colors as well as swap them back and forth.

The menu
The drop-down menu bar across the top of the window lets you select various tools and initiate processes.

The controls palette
The controls palette changes appearance depending on the tool you are using lets you customize various options each tool offers.

The toolbar
The row of buttons across the top of the screen.

The tool palette
The column of buttons down the left hand side.

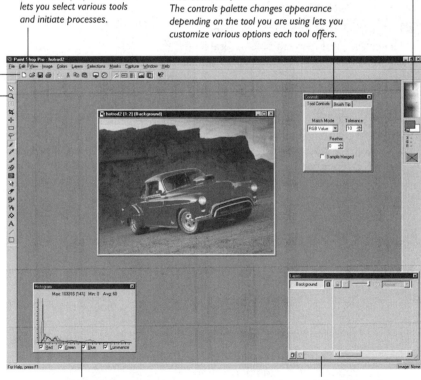

The histogram
The histogram charts how much of each color channel is distributed throughout your picture. Usually hidden from view. Explained in more detail in Chapter 6.

The layer palette
This floating toolbar lets you control, add, and edit various layers in each image.

Setting Preferences

There are some seven separate preferences areas you can set in Paint Shop Pro. Each covers a specific area of operation. From general preferences to color management, you can go a long way toward customizing Paint Shop Pro to work just the way you want.

To set Undo preferences:

1. Choose File>Preferences>General Program Preferences. The dialog opens first to the Undo preferences (**Figure 2.2**).

2. The Undo feature of Paint Shop Pro lets you undo what you just did if you decide you made a mistake. Undo takes up disk space, and you may want to not activate it on a system low in hard-drive space.

3. If you want Undo available, check the Enable the Undo System box. To disable it uncheck this box.

4. If you enable the Undo system, you can limit how much disk space it uses by checking the Limit Undo Disk Usage box and then setting the number of megabytes of hard drive space for each open image. **Note:** This number is *not* the exact number of undos you will have—it's merely the amount of space used. A really large image might only allow 5 or 10 undos if set to 20MB, whereas a smaller image might allow up to 60 undos at the same setting.

✔ Tip

■ You can limit the number of specific steps undoable per image by checking the Limit Undo to X Steps Per Open Image box.

5. Checking the Compress Undo Information box lets you fit more undo information into a smaller amount of hard drive space, but the program will operate slower.

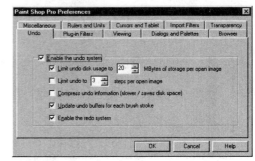

Figure 2.2 The Undo Preferences dialog box.

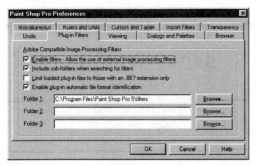

Figure 2.3 The Plug-in Filters Preferences dialog box.

6. Checking the Update undo buffers for each brush stroke forces a save for each new brush stroke as a separate, undoable step. Unchecked, it simply saves groups of brush strokes as one full step.

✔ Tip

■ If you plan to do a lot of hand drawing, check the Undo buffers for each brush stroke option.

To set Plug-in Filters preferences:

1. Choose **File>Preferences>General Program Preferences**. Click on the Plug-in Filters Tab (**Figure 2.3**).

2. To enable Paint Shop Pro to use external Abobe format filters, check the Enable Filters checkbox. When Paint Shop Pro looks for compatible filters it goes through directories on your machine to find all the compatible filters.

3. If you want to limit Paint Shop Pro to only load plug-ins that have filename extensions beginning with .8B, check the Limited Loaded Plug-In Files checkbox.

4. Checking Enable Plug-In Automatic File Format Identification forces Paint Shop Pro to read file formats supplied as plug-ins. Some plug-ins have special dialog boxes or displays that run when you're loading them. To disable this, uncheck this box.

5. Below the options are three text boxes titled Folders 1, 2, and 3. Each has a browse button to the right.

   This is where you set the folders/directories Paint Shop Pro will search to find plug-ins you've stored on your machine. The browse button brings up a dialog box where you can identify the folder containing plug-ins. You can set up to three folders. For more on plug-in filters, see Chapter 9.

SETTING PREFERENCES

To set Viewing options:

1. Choose File>Preferences>General Program Preferences and click the Viewing tab (**Figure 2.4**).

2. To automatically resize a Window around the image when zooming in, check the Fit window to image when zooming in checkbox. To resize to fit around the image when zooming out, check the Fit window to image when zooming out checkbox.

3. Next, set what Paint Shop Pro does when it loads in or initiates a new image. Choose to automatically set a zoom size or to display the image at a 1:1 ratio.

4. Check the Fit window to image checkbox if you want the window to wrap around an image after you resize it. The Auto size checkbox makes Paint Shop Pro zoom out from images you enlarge.

To set Dialogs and Palettes preferences:

1. Choose File>Preferences>General Program Preferences and click on the Palettes tab (**Figure 2.5**)

2. Paint Shop Pro 5 uses its own superior color picker. To use the standard Windows color picker instead, check the Use standard Windows color picker checkbox.

3. If you're running at a very high resolution or want to look at larger text and icons when running Paint Shop Pro check Display large text and icons on palettes.

4. Windows offers two styles of toolbars. One where the icons sit as 3-D boxes on the toolbar (**Figure 2.6a**) and a second style where they lie flat on the toolbar (**Figure 2.6b**). Checking the Display flat style toolbars enables that style; leaving it unchecked displays the 3-D boxes style.

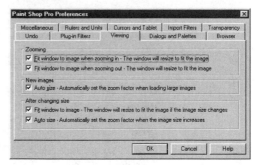

Figure 2.4 The Viewing Options dialog box.

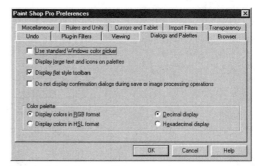

Figure 2.5 Dialogs and Palettes preferences.

Figure 2.6 The two styles of toolbars.

Figure 2.6a

Figure 2.6b

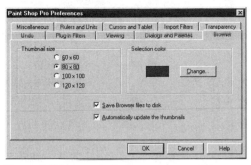

Figure 2.7 Browser preferences.

5. Make sure Do not display confirmation dialogs during save or image processing operations is unchecked. This is a dangerous option we recommend only savvy users check.

If you do check it, Paint Shop Pro does not ask you to confirm operations like overwriting saved images before performing them. Turning off confirmation speeds up your workflow but can be costly if you accidentally overwrite or irreversibly change something.

6. The Color Palette options let you set options for the color palette. To display color values in RGB or HSL choose the appropriate radio button. To display the actual values as either decimal or in hexadecimal choose the appropriate radio button. The hexadecimal setting is mostly useful for Web design.

To set Browser preferences:

1. Choose **File>Preferences>General Program Preferences** and then click on the Browser tab (**Figure 2.7**).

2. When you run the thumbnail browser you can have it display thumbnails in sizes from 60 x 60 to 120 x 120. Set thumbnail size to the size you like.

3. To select the color to designate thumbnails, click on the Change button in the Selection color area.

4. It can take awhile to display all the graphic files in a directory the first time it is browsed. To cut down that time Paint Shop Pro creates an index file that speeds subsequent browsing of that folder. If you want it to save these files for speedier browsing, check the Save Browser files to disk checkbox.

5. The Automatically update the thumbnails preference, when checked, forces Paint

Shop Pro to redo the browser file each time you save or delete or modify an image in the currently browsed folder.

To set Miscellaneous preferences:

1. Choose File>Preferences>General Program Preferences and then click the Miscellaneous tab (**Figure 2.8**).

2. The File menu displays the last few image files worked with. To expand this number, increase the number in the Recent File Listing box.

✔ Tip

- Changes to recent file list settings will not take effect until Paint Shop Pro is restarted.

3. The Tolerance to Background Color setting controls how much variance background colors in an image can have. This can be set from 0 to 200 percent. At 0, only perfectly matched pixels are considered transparent. At 200, all pixels are considered transparent. The default is 10.

4. If you tend to open up lots of images or create new ones in every working session of Paint Shop Pro, at the end of a session you may have lots of junk images or scraps.

   When you quit the program, unsaved imagery causes Paint Shop Pro to ask you if you want to save changes for every image. If you don't want to be asked this, check the Do not ask to save changes on Window Close All checkbox.

✔ Tip

- Enabling this Do not ask... option could cause you to lose something you meant to save after all.

5. If you don't care about being asked upon exiting of Paint Shop Pro if you want to empty the clipboard, check the Do not ask to empty clipboard on exit option.

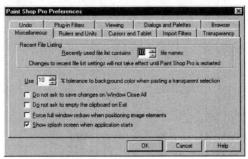

Figure 2.8 Miscellaneous preferences.

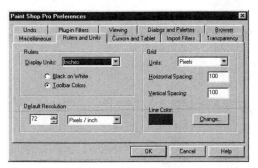

Figure 2.9 The Rulers and Units preferences.

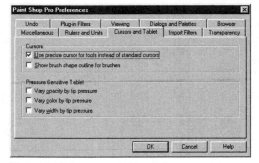

Figure 2.10 Cursor and Tablet preferences.

6. To skip the splash screen when you start up, leave Show splash screen when application starts unchecked.

To set Rulers and Units preferences:

1. Choose File>Preferences>General Program Preferences) and click on the Rulers and Units tab (**Figure 2.9**).

2. The first preference setting, Rulers lets you control how rulers and grids are displayed.

3. Set the color of the rulers to either Black on White or match whatever color the toolbars are.

4. Set the Default Resolution by specifying how many pixels per inch or per centimeter the program should use as a default. The usual default is 72 ppi.

5. Set the units the grid uses for measurement (pixels, inches, or centimeters), set the spacing attributes, and finally select the line color. The Change button activates a dialog box to choose a color.

To set Cursor and Tablet preferences:

1. Choose File>Preferences>General Program Preferences and click the Cursors and Tablet tab (**Figure 2.10**).

2. Two preferences control cursor look. The Use precise cursor for tools instead of standard cursor checkbox lets you change the cursor to a different shape that is easier to get pixel-perfect positioning. However, you lose all the visual cues that are built into the standard cursor (e.g. a +/- sign when you are in adding or subtracting mode while making a selection).

3. The Show brush shape outline option, if checked, makes Paint Shop Pro display the outer limits of the paintbrush shown while you paint.

4. If you install and use a pressure sensitive tablet you can check either Vary opacity by tip pressure or Vary color by tip pressure. More details on tablets in Chapter 3.

To set Import Filters preferences:

1. Choose File>Preferences>General Program Preferences and click the Import Filters tab (**Figure 2.11**).

2. Aldus created the filter format used as the Windows standard for file import filters. When checked, this box makes sure that Paint Shop Pro adheres to the standard.

3. The INI Section box lets you state at which heading in your WIN.INI file should it look for this information. Unless you are a most experienced user, leave this stuff alone.

To set Transparency preferences:

1. Choose File>Preferences>General Program Preferences and click the Transparency tab (**Figure 2.12**).

2. The transparency feature of Paint Shop Pro controls the background color of the transparency grid that shows transparent areas of an image are displayed with no background.

3. To the right of the preference settings is a preview picture of the grid used. You may define the Grid Size in the Grid Size using the drop down list. (your choices are tiny, small, medium and large)

4. The Grid Colors dialog lets you set the color of the checkerboard pattern. Click on the Scheme drop down menu and choose any of the available schemes.

There are three file formats that you can set preference for in Paint Shop Pro. You can also set which file formats are directly associated with Paint Shop Pro.

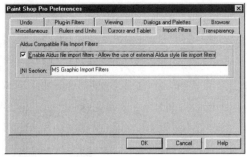

Figure 2.11 Import Filters preferences.

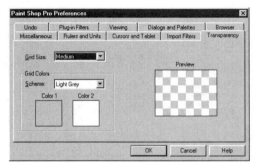

Figure 2.12 Transparency preferences.

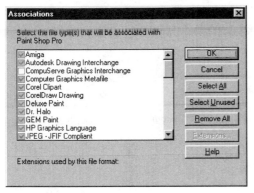

Figure 2.13 File Association dialog box.

File associations in Windows are what allow you to click on a file and have the program that can edit or view it automatically run and view the file. By associating files with programs we are able to more quickly load and edit individual files.

To set File Association preferences:

1. Choose File>Preferences>Set File Association Preferences. The Set File Associations dialog box appears (**Figure 2.13**).

✔ Tip

■ You are automatically asked to select file types for association when installing Paint Shop Pro. If other programs supercede these associations, or you want to change some, you need to set the associations again using these preferences.

2. On the left side of the dialog box is a list of all the major file types Paint Shop Pro 5 supports. You may check the checkbox of each file you want Paint Shop Pro to be the associated viewer/editor for. You can also quickly use the Select All or Select None buttons as well.

3. If you want to select all formats no other program has claimed yet check the Unused button.

4. Click OK when Done.

Customizing Toolbars

As we said earlier, you'll use several toolbars in Paint Shop Pro. The tool palette (on the left side of the screen) lets you quickly select the painting, drawing, and selecting tools you need. The toolbar (at the top of the screen) allows for quick access to new files, saving, loading, and more. You can't modify the tool palette, but you can modify the toolbar.

To customize the toolbar:

1. Choose **File>Preferences>Customize Toolbar**. The Customize Toolbar dialog box appears (**Figure 2.14**).

2. You see two lists of icons. On the left is a list of all available buttons you may choose from. On the right is the current configuration for the toolbar.

3. Select an item on the left and then choose Add, double-click it, or drag it over to the right window to place it on the toolbar.

✔ Tip

- If you click Add or doubleclick a tool, the program appends that button to the end of the toolbar. Dragging it over lets you drop it down exactly where you'd like the item to be placed on the toolbar.

4. Once an item is on the toolbar you may drag it up or down the list to place it exactly where you'd like it.

5. To remove an item, highlight it on the right and either doubleclick it, click the Remove button, or drag it out of the list.

6. The separator button lets you place a blank space on your toolbar.

✔ Tip

- To reset the toolbar to its default configuration click the Reset button.

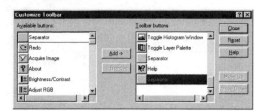

Figure 2.14 Customize toolbar dialog box.

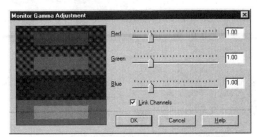

Figure 2.15 The Set Monitor Gamma dialog box.

Monitor Gamma

You can adjust your monitor's gamma level. The results of improving your Monitor Gamma can be better display of color levels and gradation for your display.

To Set Monitor Gamma:

1. Choose File>Preferences>Set Monitor Gamma.

2. The Monitor Gamma Adjustment dialog box will appear (**Figure 2.15**).

3. You'll see four color rectangles: Red, Green, Blue, Gray. Each box has a solid middle section and outer dithered edge.

4. On the right side are sliders that adjust the Gamma levels of the color. The object is to slide the sliders until the two areas of each rectangle are of equal brightness. At that point you've calibrated the Monitor Gamma.

✔ Tip

■ Use Link Channels to move all three sliders in unison. When you need to fine tune each one, uncheck the Link checkbox.

MONITOR GAMMA

Creating, Saving, and Opening Images

It's a snap to work with images in Paint Shop Pro.

To create a new image:

1. Click the New Image button on the toolbar, choose **File>New Image**, or press Ctrl+N.

2. The New Image dialog box appears (**Figure 2.16**).

3. Set the Width and Height in the unit value presented in the drop-down box.

4. Choose a measurement value (Pixels, Inches or Centimeters).

5. For image resolution you may also set the number of pixels per inch or centimeter. First set the number in the box just below Height and Width. Then choose the measurement ratio.

6. In the Image Characteristics area set the background color of the new image and the bit depth (for more on bit depth see Chapter 6).

✔ Tip

■ As you enter information the box will display at the bottom the total amount of RAM needed to display the image. This is not the file size when saved but the current memory needed to show it on the screen.

7. Click OK when you've got the right setup. Note that almost all these image characteristics can be adjusted once you've begun working on it through other individual processses.

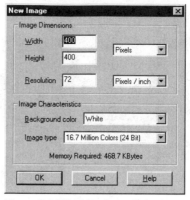

Figure 2.16 The New Image dialog box.

CREATING, SAVING, AND OPENING IMAGES

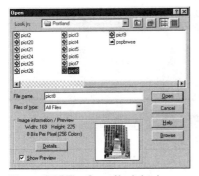

Figure 2.17 The Open file dialog box.

Figure 2.18 The Browse Image File dialog box.

To save an image:

There are a number of saving options—enough that we've got an entire chapter on it. Please refer to Chapter 12.

To load an Image:

1. Click on the Open File Icon or choose **File>Open** or press Ctrl+O.

2. The Open File Dialog will appear (**Figure 2.17**). Note that this works just like almost every other common Windows program you're familiar with, but some additions are apparent.

3. Type the filename in the File Name text box or choose it from the file window. Use the drop-down list at the top to move through various drives and directories.

✔ Tips

■ You may limit your files viewed to a specific type using the Files of Type drop down list.

■ To browse all the files in the current directory in the visual image browser, press the Browse button.

4. At the bottom of the box is a preview window. This window will show a preview of the image, if available, if you check the Show Preview checkbox.

5. When you find the file you want to load click the Open button or press Enter.

To use the image browser:

1. Choose **File>Browse** or press Ctrl+B or hit the Browse button in the File Open dialog box.

2. The Browse window appears and begins displaying graphics that appear in the currently set directory (**Figure 2.18**).

CREATING, SAVING, AND OPENING IMAGES

3. To set the browser to a different directory locate that directory in the directory tree displayed on the left.

4. To open an image displayed in the browser window, double-click on it.

5. To select multiple images displayed in the browser window use the Shift key to select a range or the Ctrl key to individually select images into a group.

When highlighted, click the right mouse-button to bring up the pop-up menu (**Figure 2.19**). Choose the appropriate item from the menu (Copy, Delete, Move, Rename, Information, or Open Image).

✔ Tip

■ Rename and Information don't work when multiple images are selected.

6. To see information about an image, right click on it and choose Information from the menu. An informational dialog will appear (**Figure 2.20**)

7. To rename a file select the image and right click on the mousebutton and choose rename from the menu. The rename dialog will appear (**Figure 2.21**) Type in a new name to complete the process and click **OK**.

8. When choosing Copy or Move To from the menu a dialog (**Figure 2.22**) appears, letting you choose the new directory for the copy or to move the images to.

9. When you are done using the Browse window, simply minimize or close it to discard it out of view.

Figure 2.19 The Browse pop up menu.

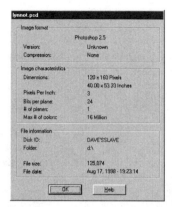

Figure 2.20 The Image Information dialog box.

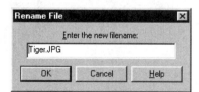

Figure 2.21 The Rename Image dialog box.

Figure 2.22 The Copy and Move To dialog box.

Figure 2.23 Full Screen Edit.

Figure 2.24 Full Screen Preview.

Figure 2.25 The Grid.

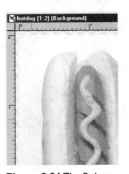

Figure 2.26 The Rulers.

Setting Your View

There are a number of quick things you can do to adjust the view you are in for editing or previewing an image.

To adjust your view for editing or previewing:

1. To set the screen to full screen edit mode (**Figure 2.23**), choose View>Full Screen Edit or Shift+A. Choose it again to turn it off.

2. To set the screen to full screen preview mode (**Figure 2.24**) choose View>Full Screen Preview or press Shift+Ctrl+A. Press Esc to return the view to normal.

3. To see the grid on the image (**Figure 2.25**) choose Grid>View or press Ctrl+Alt+G. Choose it again to turn it off.

4. To view the rulers on an image (**Figure 2.26**) choose Rulers>View. Choose it again to turn them off.

5. To choose the Toolbars to display choose View>Toolbars. The Toolbars dialog will appear (**Figure 2.27**) and you may check on or off from view any of the seven major tools or dialogs.

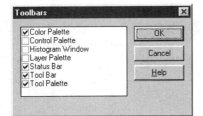

Figure 2.27 The View Toolbar dialog box.

To view image information and set creator information:

1. Choose View>Image Information or press Shift+I.

2. The Current Image Information dialog box appears (**Figure 2.28**).

3. The dialog has two tabs the first, Image Information shows a number of statistics about the image as presently created.

4. The second tab brings up the Creator Information dialog (**Figure 2.29**) here you can set key information about the title, copyright, creator and description of the image to be stored with the file. However this only is stored in the save file if you use the native .psp format.

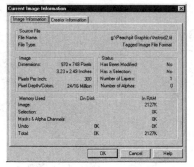

Figure 2.28 The Current Image Information dialog box.

Figure 2.29 The Creator Information dialog box.

Figure 2.30 The Tip of The Day.

Figure 2.31 The About dialog box.

Getting Help

Even with this book you might have questions—we hope not, but there are a number of ways Jasc and the Paint Shop Pro program offer to help you get the most of the package.

To get help from Paint Shop Pro and Jasc:

1. To view the Tip of the Day (**Figure 2.30**), choose Help>Tip of the Day.

   To View the built-in Help file choose Help Topics from the Help Menu. To check the Support Pages on the Jasc Web Site choose Help>Jasc Software Online>Support Pages.

2. To Send an email to technical support choose Help>Jasc Software Online>Email Technical Support. An email message with the appropriate address will be generated automatically.

3. To Check for updated versions, choose Help>Jasc Software Online>Check for Updates.

✔ Tip

- To see the version of Paint Shop Pro you are currently running, choose Help>About Paint Shop Pro. The About dialog (**Figure 2.31**) contains the version number.

4. Jasc also offers a Designer's Studio on its site that includes more tips, extra tutorials, and more. Choose Help>Jasc Software Online>Designer's Studio.

✔ Tip

- To Get Help on a specific button or menu item, choose the Help Topic button from the toolbar and select any menu item or press any button in Paint Shop Pro. The appropriate Help topic will appear.

IMAGE ACQUISITION

When it comes to using Paint Shop Pro, or any graphics package for that matter, a challenge faced by non-artists is that of developing good-looking imagery. Many new users need to learn how to handle photographs, scanned imagery, and clip art.

This chapter is designed to bring you up to speed on two very important issues: How do I get my graphics source material into Paint Shop Pro, and how do I make sure I have the right to use that imagery?

Digital Cameras

The digital camera is one of the hottest consumer products around. Giving you the ability to simply snap a photo and instantly download it into your computer, the digital camera is a powerful tool for anyone who wants a quick and easy way to get imagery onto their computer screen.

However, before you rush to the store to check out the wide variety of models now on the market, it's important to know some of the basics about digital cameras.

To buy a digital camera:

1. The first thing is to decide about two critical and related issues: cost and image resolution. The more affordable models produce images at 640 x 480 resolution and run below $400. At the next level up, the cameras create imagery at 1024 x 768 resolution and run from $600 to $1000, depending on the model, the camera's other features, and the vendor.

2. Once you've decided whether you are going to get a camera that is less than $400 or one that offers better than 640 x 480 resolution, we suggest you examine the features that differentiate cameras within a particular price range. Fortunately the Web offers a couple of sites which can help you comparison shop for digital cameras. One is C|Net's Computers.com (**www.computers.com**) shown in **Figure 3.1**, and another is Ziff Davis's Netbuyer (**www.netbuyer.com**).

3. Both services usually have reviews or comparison specifications and average prices for a range of the latest cameras. Your other options would be to check major camera stores and read reviews of the latest cameras, which tend to appear in many of the major computer magazines every six months or so.

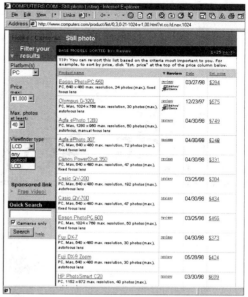

Figure 3.1 Comparing the latest digital cameras and the latest prices is a snap with Web-based comparison services like C|Net's Computers.com.

✔ Tips

- Most current digital cameras are of the point-and-shoot variety. They do not operate with fancy lenses and other features of 35mm cameras. There are digital cameras which are housed with 35mm-style camera systems, but they cost well into the thousands of dollars. Eventually they'll come down in price, but for now only a few cameras offer much more than the point-and-shoot capability.

- When considering buying a digital camera, understand that instead of film, you'll be going through a lot of batteries. Most cameras use AA batteries, and a rechargeable battery system might help save money. Many cameras also have the option of power packs, which you can use when operating the camera indoors.

- Other things to consider when purchasing a digital camera are the number of photos it can hold in memory; whether it offers removable memory cards so you can carry extra memory for storing photos (memory cards may also be referred to as digital film, or PCMCIA Cards); and whether the camera offers a built-in preview screen or power zooming.

- After you've decided on a camera, you might want to see if there are other lens offerings and accessories for it. A well-known supplier of digital camera add-on products and accessories is DC PRO (www.dcprodirect.com). They have a large range of specialty lenses you can add on to popular digital camera models, as well as extra memory cards, carrying cases, tripods and more.

Once you've obtained a digital camera, you're going to want to use it with Paint Shop Pro. The first thing to do is to install what are known as the TWAIN drivers. This is software

DIGITAL CAMERAS

that is supplied with your camera and allows it to be used with any TWAIN-compliant graphics package, such as Paint Shop Pro. The instructions for installing these drivers will come with your camera.

✔ Tip

- There are direct menu items for Kodak DC40 and Kodak DC50 cameras (see **Figure 3.2**). The drivers are standard with Paint Shop Pro 5.0.

To use your digital camera with Paint Shop Pro:

1. Once you've installed the TWAIN drivers, there are only two menu items you need to know about. They are both located under the File menu on a submenu that branches off from the Acquire menu. The Acquire (File>Import>Twain>Acquire) and Select Source (File>Import>Twain> Select Source) menu items control access to digital cameras and scanners.

    Select Source (**Figure 3.3**) brings up a menu which allows you to choose which of the installed TWAIN devices should be run when you select Acquire from the menu. Scanners and other graphics devices run off this system, so it is not uncommon to be switching back and forth a few times in a single session.

2. Once you select the TWAIN source, simply choose Acquire (File>Acquire> Acquire), and the program which lets you obtain imagery from your camera will run within Paint Shop Pro. Refer to the owner's manual that came with your camera for details on these programs, as they are all different (See **Figure 3.4**).

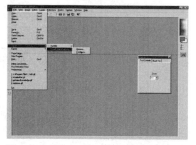

Figure 3.2 Paint Shop Pro includes native support for the popular DC40 and DC50 cameras from Kodak.

Figure 3.3 Setting the active TWAIN driver.

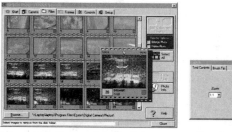

Figure 3.4 Once you've installed your TWAIN driver and selected it properly, you can acquire imagery from your camera directly within Paint Shop Pro.

✔ Tip

- You will find updated camera drivers and software on the manufacturer's Web site. If that fails to help, try running the camera software separately and saving the camera files to disk. You can then load them into Paint Shop Pro. Unfortunately, sometimes TWAIN drivers and scanner or camera software may not run perfectly within another program. Report problems to the manufacturer, as it is usually the fault of TWAIN drivers, not Paint Shop Pro.

DIGITAL CAMERAS

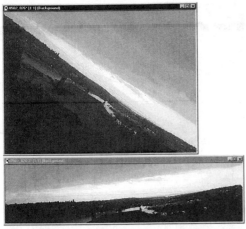

Figure 3.5 Rotation of graphics lets you take advantage of angles when shooting with a digital camera.

Figure 3.6 A digital camera makes capturing textures a snap.

Digital Camera Tips

Too much or too little light will cause pictures to wash out or be pitch black. We find that for outdoor shots, the optimal times to shoot are at sunrise, in the late afternoon, and on partly cloudy days.

To use light to your advantage:

When indoors, sometimes it helps to set up a white backdrop for your shots. Taping some solid white paper (found at a local art supply store) to the wall and on a table against the wall can help make it easy to cut out photographed objects from the background when you're using Paint Shop Pro.

To experiment with angles:

Because Paint Shop Pro lets you rotate imagery, try fitting imagery you want to capture into the picture by taking pictures at odd angles. For example, in **Figure 3.5** we took a skyline shot at sunset along the longest line in the camera (diagonally). Then we filled in the rest after rotating it to a level view, and ended up with what looks like a longer look of the horizon of Seattle.

To capture textures:

You can use photographed textures as fills and build a library of photorealistic brushes and backgrounds. Because with a digital camera you can easily take multiple photos, shoot the same texture at several different distances as shown in **Figure 3.6**.

To create panoramic shots:

You can take multiple shots and stitch them together to create extra-long landscape photos. Keeping the camera very carefully still and at precisely the same height, turn your body slightly as you snap each photo to continually capture a wider area. Be sure to overlap the photos so that you can line them up later on.

DIGITAL CAMERA TIPS

Figure 3.7 shows a stitched together photo of our friend John Hoyt's backyard garden. Five photos were taken this way and overlapped to create this image.

✔ Tip

■ If you want to take incredibly good photos this way, get a tripod. There are special virtual reality photography tripods made by Kaidan (**www.kaidan.com**) which are used by many professionals for these types of stitched together wide-angle photos.

To maximize available resolution:

When photographing a subject, decide ahead of time whether you will want to cut out the subject from the background later on. If that's the case, fit as much of the subject in the photo as possible, without regard for the background. Because digital cameras only offer a finite number of pixels, you want to devote as many of them to the subject as possible to maximize the resolution.

Figure 3.7 We took five photos to create a wide-angle view of our friend's backyard garden.

35mm or Advanced Photo System Cameras

There are two major traditional camera systems out on the market today: 35mm, which the majority of professionals in the industry and many hobbyists use, and what is known as the Advanced Photo System (APS) cameras. Kodak markets its APS cameras under the brand name Advantix, and most other major camera companies offer their own versions of the APS cameras.

What makes APS interesting to casual photographers and users of computers is that the format has special technologies built into it that allow for easy conversion into computer graphics you can use in Paint Shop Pro. In addition, APS supports three different picture sizes, and can digitally encode information with the picture such as caption, date, and time. The downside to APS cameras is that they're not 35mm, and thus the photo quality isn't as good. Although APS wouldn't be the choice of a serious hobbyist or professional, for the rest of us APS is an appealing format.

There are two methods you can use to develop your pictures into graphics. You can have your photos developed and scanned for you by a development lab (more on this later) or you can purchase a film scanner.

✔ Tip

- When buying a camera for taking photos and converting them to graphics, most hard-core camera-users will tell you to buy a 35mm. However, given the costs, and the purposes for which you'll be using it, a good Advance Photo System camera may suit you just as well.

Traditional Scanners

One of the most popular ways to acquire imagery for graphics work is to scan it in using a flatbed scanner, such as Hewlett Packard's ScanJet. There are many popular models, including Agfa (a favorite among graphic artists), Microtek (well-liked by production folks), and Umax.

Flatbed scanners vary greatly in their capabilities, so be sure you get what you want. There are distinct differences in features that you get when buying low-end scanners (usually under $300–$400), mid-range scanners (which run from $500–$1,000), and top-end scanners (which run over $1,000). Most of the difference in capability has to do with the quality of the resolution. So before you buy one, make sure you understand the differences among the three levels of scanners available.

✔ Tip

- Many users will do fine with a low-end or mid-range scanner. Most major models perform well, and the major computing magazines all run scanner roundups for those of you who want to inspect more detailed reviews of the latest models.

Slide/Film and Photo Scanners

Most people are familiar with traditional flatbed scanners, but a newer style of scanner is becoming widely used by pros and hobbyists alike.

By scanning film strips directly (or high-quality slides) they can ensure a much better scan. In addition, you needn't have the pictures printed to scan them (if you use film scanning); instead, just have the film developed and then scan.

Slide/Film scanners run from $800–$2,000 for top- quality scanners capable of 2000–2700 DPI. If you plan on scanning APS film, you will need a specific APS film scanner or one that accepts an attachment for scanning APS film.

Fuji sells the AS-1, an APS-only scanner; it's fairly inexpensive but offers lower resolution than other film scanners. That makes it a good choice for someone who only has a casual interest and isn't using a 35mm camera. In terms of other film scanners, Olympus offers the ES line of film scanners which feature an APS attachment. Most of the newest APS scanners also let you modify the save elements on the film—not the pictures, but any of the other encoded information that was saved on a small magnetic strip than runs alongside the film. This lets you add captions, set dates, etc.

In terms of 35mm slide or film scanners, Polaroid, Kodak, Minolta, and Olympus are among a number of major film companies offering products.

Photoscanners are a hybrid of traditional scanners. Usually produced for a lower cost than full flatbed scanners, photoscanners are inexpensive ways to scan in 3.5" x 5" and 4 x 6" photos you've had developed. Some computers even have them built in. Overall, these scanners are best for casual users who aren't terribly worried about developing high-quality scans. With their low price and a quality good enough for homepages and grandparents, they're a good option for people who take lots of family vacation photos.

To buy a scanner:

1. Decide on your budget and the features that are important to you. The most critical issues to consider are the image resolution (DPI) and whether you will be scanning lots of documents as well as images (in which case a scanner that excels at text conversion may win out over ones that don't).

   Slide/film scanners might be best. They offer enhanced quality for the cost but can't scan images other than slides or film. If all you're going to do is scan film and slides, then a flatbed may be inferior. Low-end, home users may be best with just a photo-scanner.

2. Make sure you have space in your machine for the scanner! Most scanners require a separate card to be installed in an open expansion slot on your computer. Be sure you know the port/card requirements for your scanner ahead of time.

3. Check the major computer magazines and computer-magazine Web sites. About every six months someone does a large roundup of the latest models.

4. When you do purchase the product, visit the company's Web site to check the availability of updated TWAIN drivers and software for the product.

Figure 3.8 PhotoNet stores your images and lets you sort through the thumbnails on the Web.

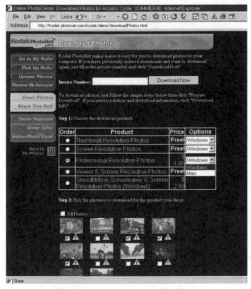

Figure 3.9 PhotoNet lets you download medium-resolution versions of your pictures for free. You can also download high-resolution versions of the photos, or order printouts, for a small fee.

PhotoNet/Photo Scanning Services

The advent of the Internet, America Online (AOL), and the Web has made it simple for people to send photos back and forth electronically. PhotoNet is a service developed by Picturevision, a small software company. PhotoNet has licensed to Kodak, AOL, and others a system which allows people to have scanned photos sent to them online.

To use PhotoNet:

1. Shoot a roll of film with your camera and take the film to a participating PhotoNet development shop.

2. Fill out the form and make sure to check "PhotoNet development," or write it in if there isn't a checkbox on the envelope.

3. The developer will take the film, scan the photos into a high-resolution format, and upload them to the Web. When this is completed, the system sends you an e-mail message.

4. Scanned photos are available 24–48 hours after drop-off. When you get your e-mail notification, the photos are available by logging onto a special Web site (**Figure 3.8**), or keyword area in the case of AOL. There you enter in your name, password and claim number for the film you dropped off.

5. After inputting the information you will be greeted by thumbnail versions of the photos (**Figure 3.9**). Photos can be instantly downloaded at a 640 x 480 resolution for free, or you can obtain much higher resolutions (usually for a small extra download fee).

6. In the case of Kodak's PhotoNet (www.photonet.kodak.com), you can order reprints or get T-shirts or mugs made.

Kodak has pioneered the most visible rollout of PhotoNet, but other manufacturers are expected to join in. In addition, Kodak and AOL have partnered to create Your Pictures on AOL, which is a similar service to be built into AOL's client software.

✔ Tips

■ Aside from PhotoNet, many other graphics service bureaus exist which will scan your photos for you for a fee. Someday, getting scans back via e-mail or the Web may be the only process we use to develop film.

■ A popular place to have film developed online is Seattle Filmworks (**Figure 3.10**). You mail your film to Seattle Filmworks, and they develop and send back many types of prints; they can send back scans, photo CDs, and more. You can find them on the Web at **www.seattlefilmworks.com**.

Figure 3.10 Seattle Filmworks is one of the oldest Web-based photo developers around. Send them your rolls of film, and they'll e-mail back scanned versions.

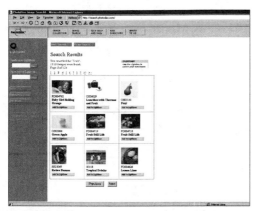

Figure 3.11 Clip-art companies are on the Web.

Figure 3.12 The Xoom Web site offers clip art for free.

Clip Art Vendors

A number of major vendors offer clip art for sale. We like the following places:

Artville
www.artville.com

Rubberball
www.rubberball.com

Photoessentials
www.phtoessentials.canon.com.au

Goodshoot
www.goodshoot.com

PhotoDisc
www.photodisc.com

Master Series
www.masterseries.com

Cyberphoto
www.cyberphoto.com

Image Club
www.imageclub.com

John Foxx Images
www.johnfoxx.com

Corbis
www.corbis.com

Diamar Interactive
www.diamar.com

CD and Web-Based Clip Art

Don't have any images of your own to scan or a camera to take pictures? Lots of people turn to ready-made clip art. The demand for clip art has been increasing, and so have the offerings. A number of major companies, like PhotoDisc, have debuted professional and affordable images and CD-ROM collections.

Some companies are now selling clip art directly over the Web for instant image-by-image access (**Figure 3.11**). This makes it easy to buy and use only the art you need. Previously you might pay $50–$200 for a CD containing 100 images, only to end up using one or two.

In addition, many people have started up free clip-art collections on the Internet. One such company is Xoom (**www.xoom.com**), which offers lots of free and useful clips for people building Web pages (**Figure 3-12**).

A note of caution, however: be sure that the site really is offering the art for free use, and that it is authorized to do so. It's not unheard of for fly-by-night sites to put up imagery and offer it as free for public use, when in actuality it is not. Be sure to look through the site to see if it is reputable and to read what specific rights they grant you for the imagery (any good site will have this information prominently placed). If you have any doubts, that should be enough to avoid using it.

Tablets

If you're a decent freehand artist you may already have or be thinking about purchasing a drawing tablet. Paint Shop Pro supports drawing tablets, and if you are going to use the product a lot even a small tablet may prove to be a more productive way to use the program than a mouse. You can also use tablets to trace over line art as well. If you're going to do hand illustrations in Paint Shop Pro, then a tablet is the way to go. Note also that Chapter 2 describes some specific preference settings that apply to using tablets in Paint Shop Pro.

There are several types of tablets available, but by far the most popular are those made by Wacom, Inc. (**www.wacom.com**). Wacom offers two models of pads. The ArtPad II series (under $150–$200) is a low-end pad which measures 4 x 5 inches and is great for casual users and kids. The other product is Wacom's ArtZ series of tablets, which run in size from 6 x 8 ($350) up to 12 x 18 ($700).

With every tablet, Wacom also includes PenTools, a set of special plug-ins. These plug-ins provide special paint tools which work specifically with these pressure-sensitive tablets.

SELECTIONS

The selection tools are some of the most important and useful tools Paint Shop Pro provides. In order to use the special filters and adjusting tools, you must first have a selected area to work with.

In this chapter, we discuss how to create a selection, how to increase a selection's size, how to undo a selection, and many more ways to use the selection tools. First, though, we cover all the features listed in the Selections drop-down menu and explain their functions.

Selection Basics

When you create a selection, you have the following choices: Contract, Expand, Feather, Grow Selection, Select Similar, and Transparent Color.

When a selection is contracted, the marquee moves in and becomes smaller by the number of pixels specified.

Expanding a selection simply moves the marquee out the number of pixels desired.

Feathering moves the marquee out just like when it is expanded. The difference between expanding and feathering is that feathering blends the pixels on the outer edge of the selection.

Grow Selection does just what it says: the selected areas on the screen multiply. Not only does your current selection remain, but additional selections appear on the image.

When you choose Select Similar, the colors that make up the current selection are used to select the same colors in other places on the image that contain those color pixels.

The last option in Modify is Transparent Color. This deselects all of the pixels in the selection that contain the chosen colors.

The following step-by-step instructions should make it easy to use all of the functions of the selection tools. We begin with some basics of zooming in and out of an image, as this can be extremely helpful when creating selections.

To zoom in and out of an image:

1. Select the Zoom tool 🔍.

To make it a little easier to create a selection, you may want to zoom in or out of the picture. Zooming in makes the image bigger, so the edges are easier to trace around, as seen in **Figure 4.1**. Zoom out to

SELECTION BASICS

Figure 4.1 Zooming in makes it easier to create selections correctly.

get back to the normal size. If the picture is large, you may want to zoom out to make the image smaller. This allows you to view more of the image in one frame, and makes creating a selection more manageable.

2. To zoom in, click on the area of the image to zoom in on with the left mouse button.

3. To zoom out, click on the image with the right mouse button. It's that simple.

✔ Tip

- If your mouse has a middle wheel, this can be used to zoom in and out. Rolling up zooms in, and rolling down zooms out.

SELECTION BASICS

Creating a Selection

There are four different ways to create a selection. In this section, we go over the basics of using each one.

To make a basic selection:

1. On the tool palette there is a rectangular-shaped icon, which you can select to activate the basic selection tool ⌷. This tool is useful when you want to make a selection of a specific geometric shape. The setting on this tool can be changed from a rectangle to a square, an ellipse, or a circle.

2. Once you've activated the tool, you can change the shape of the selection style by choosing from a list that is available on the control panel (**Figure 4.2**).(If it is not visible, press O on the keyboard)

3. The control panel allows you to change the shape of the selection tool, the feathering and whether the antialias is active or not (if the control panel is not shown, press O on the keyboard). You can set the feathering here instead of going to the Selections menu.

4. The antialias setting is similar to feathering, but it allows for an even higher degree of accuracy. Antialias partially fills the pixels along the edge of the selection, making them semi-transparent. The result is a smoother edge on the selection. (Antialias has to be checked before making the selection. Afterwards, it is too late, and checking it does not affect the image.)

5. When the shape and other options have been selected, the selection can be made.

6. The cursor changes when it is dragged across the image. The cursor becomes either a plus sign alone, or a plus sign

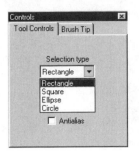

Figure 4.2 The control panel for the basic selection tool lets you choose several different selection shapes.

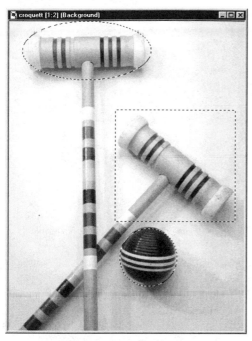

Figure 4.3 It's easy to make different styles of selections using the basic selection tool. Here we've used a circle, an ellipse, and a rectangle in our selection.

Figure 4.4 The control panel for the Freehand selection tool.

with the shape you have chosen for the selection.

7. Click and drag the mouse from the starting corner to the ending corner for a rectangle or square. For the circle and the ellipse, start in the center of what will be selected. A line forms as the mouse moves across the intended selection area. **Figure 4.3** shows several basic selections made using the different shapes available with the basic selection tool.

8. When the selection is the desired size, release the mouse button. The borders of the selection become a marquee (sometimes affectionately referred to as the "marching ants"), and you are now ready to perform commands and processes on that item.

✔ Tip

■ You can activate a dialog box to enter the exact pixel position for the corners of the selection. Double-click on the selections tool, and in the boxes labeled Left, Right, Top and Bottom, enter the pixel position for the corners of the selection. When you click OK, the dialog box closes and the selection is created.

To use the Freehand tool:

1. The Freehand tool is used to create irregularly shaped selections. It is activated by clicking on the lasso-shaped Freehand tool. There are three choices with this tool: Freehand, Point to Point and Smart Edge. We discuss Freehand first.

2. The control panel should be visible (**Figure 4.4**), and should give you the options for Selection Type, Feathering and Antialias, which we went over earlier. There is also a Sample Merged checkbox; this allows a selection to be made to all of the layers at one time, not just the current layer.

CREATING A SELECTION

3. Move the cursor over the image, with the Freehand tool selected. The lasso image appears with a plus sign next to it. This means it is ready to draw the selection.

4. Click the mouse button and drag the mouse to create the desired selection. The boundary line can cross over itself— only the enclosed image will be part of the selected area.

5. Let go of the mouse button when finished. (If the starting and ending points do not meet, a straight line is drawn between them to complete the selection.) **Figure 4.5** shows an image we outlined with a selection, using the Freehand selection tool.

Figure 4.5 The Freehand selection tool in action.

To use the Point to Point tool:

1. The Point to Point tool is found under Selection Type on the control panel when the Freehand selection tool is active. This is useful when you want to create a selection that is outlined by connected straight lines.

2. Click on the Freehand tool. Select Point to Point under Selection Type on the control panel. Set all of the desired options.

3. The same lasso with the plus sign appears when the cursor is moved across the image. Click on the point where the first line should begin; the middle of the plus sign is the target.

You do not need to hold down the mouse button. A line forms from the original point to where you drag the mouse and click again for the second point.

4. The lines continue to be drawn from point to point, with every click becoming an anchor point. If you decide that an anchor point is in the wrong place, hit the Delete key and it is erased back to the previous anchor point. The line is still active, and you can click for another anchor point.

Figure 4.6 The Point to Point selection tool in action.

5. In order to end the drawing of the selection, you must double-click the final point or right-click on the mouse. This ends the formation of the lines, and a marquee is created for your selection. **Figure 4.6** shows an image that was selected using the Point to Point selection tool.

To use the Smart Edge tool:

1. This is the last of the Freehand tool choices. It is best used for selecting a border between two areas of contrasting color or light.

2. Click on the Freehand tool and select Smart Edge under Selection Type on the control panel. Set the desired options.

3. The cursor turns into a lasso with a plus sign. The middle of the plus sign is the target. Click on a starting point. A rectangular box forms as the mouse is dragged across the image.

4. Click on an ending point or anchor point. The rectangular box turns into a line that follows the edge of the section selected. The line falls between the light and dark areas.

5. To remove the previous anchor point, use the Delete key.

6. When the selection is completed, double-click or right-click with the mouse, and the selection becomes surrounded by a marquee. Everything inside the border is selected, even if the border you draw crosses over itself.

CREATING A SELECTION

To use the Magic Wand selection tool:

1. The Magic Wand selection tool ✐ is useful when you need to select very specific areas in an image. It also works to snap the selection marquee around images based on color characteristics. This makes it ideal to use to quickly select irregularly shaped imagery that is all of a similar color or brightness.

2. There are four different values that can be used to determine the type of selection desired. You can choose them from the control panel that is associated with the Magic Wand selection tool (**Figure 4.7**). They are RGB Value, Hue, Brightness and All Pixels. Start using this tool by selecting it from the tool bar, or from the menu.

3. If it's not up, activate the control panel palette for the Magic Wand. Note the drop-down list titled Match Mode. On this list are four values for the Magic Wand tool, which control the Match Mode. The Match Mode determines exactly which criteria are used when the Magic Wand selects groups of similar pixels. There are four possibilities:

   RGB: Selects areas that match only the RGB color values of the original point area.

   Hue: Selects only the pixels that match the hue of the area which is clicked.

   Brightness: Selects areas nearby that have the same level of brightness as the selected area.

   All Pixels: Selects pixels that are similar and nearby the original selected area.

✔ Tip

- Note that transparent areas of an image can't be selected using the Magic Wand.

  Also on the control panel for the Magic Wand is the Tolerance setting. The number

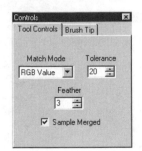

Figure 4.7 The control panel for the Magic Wand selection tool.

Figure 4.8a The Magic Wand tool, using a lower tolerance setting.

Figure 4.8b The Magic Wand tool, using a higher tolerance setting.

placed here determines how much variance is allowed in the Match Mode settings when the Magic Wand looks for similarly styled pixels.

For example, if the tolerance is set at a low number, such as 3, it does not select very much of the surrounding area from the original point you click on. If the tolerance is set higher (the top setting is 200), a larger number of pixels are selected. You can see the difference in the size of the selections based on tolerance settings in **Figures 4.8a** and **4.8b**.

4. After you set the options, drag the cursor over the image, and it changes to a wand icon with a plus sign.

5. Use the center of the plus sign for the target, and click on the area to be selected. From this point outward, the computer searches for adjacent pixels that match the color characteristics and fall within the tolerance setting you've chosen.

6. If the desired area is not completely selected, then hold down the Shift key, and click elsewhere on the image in regions you want to add to the original selection. This can be done repeatedly until the marquee surrounds the entire area you want to select.

✔ Tip

■ To select an entire layer, simply click the button of the layer to be made current. (Layers are covered more extensively in Chapter 5). In the Selections menu click Select All. A marquee appears around the whole image on that layer.

To add or subtract from a selection:

1. Create an initial selection using one of the selection tools. Once you've created an initial selection, you may need to add to the selection or subtract additional areas from it.

2. To add to the selection, hold down Shift while the selection tool is still active. A plus sign appears next to the selection tool, indicating that you are ready to add to the selected areas of an image. Click on the areas that still need to be selected. Continue to hold down the Shift key while additional selections are being made.

3. To delete from a selection, do the same as you would to add to a selection, except hold down the Control key. Make sure that you are positioned inside a selected area. Then drag the mouse as you would to make a selection; this subtracts the areas you do not want to keep in the selection.

4. **Figures 4.9a** and **4.9b** show selections around the base of a tennis racket. However, the selection in **Figure 4-9a** is not as perfect as we'd like. So by adding in areas and subtracting other areas, we can get a selection like that seen in **Figure 4.9b**, which is much closer to the object we're trying to select.

To deselect an entire selection:

From the Selections menu, choose Select None (**Selections>Select None** or Control-D), or when using a selection tool, simply click on the right mouse button.

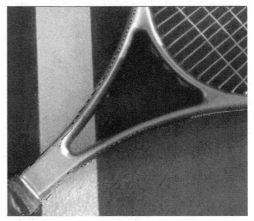

Figure 4.9a The original rough selection.

Figure 4.9b After it's been tightened up, using adding and subtracting from a selection.

Macaroni & Cheese

Figure 4.10 Expanding a selection.

Figure 4.11 This screen shows the difference between a selection which was simply cut, and one which was feathered before being cut.

Selection Options

We explain the function of these tools in the beginning of this chapter. Now we go into more detail about how to use them.

To contract a selection:

1. Select an area with one of the selection tools.

2. Under the Selections menu, choose Modify, Contract.

3. Select the number of pixels that the selected area should be contracted. The maximum number of pixels you can choose is 100.

To expand a selection:

1. Create a selection using one of the selection tools.

2. Under the Selections menu, choose Modify, Expand.

3. Select the amount to be expanded in pixels, up to 100. **Figure 4.10** shows an expanded selection around text.

To feather a selection:

1. Create a selection area with one of the selection tools.

2. Under the Selections menu, choose Modify, Feather or Control-H. The Feather dialog box appears.

3. The Feather spin control sets the feather amount. A setting of 0 creates the sharpest edges. The feather can be set up to 200 for the softest edges, although 200 might be a bit much for most projects. In general, we find that the best feathers are usually 2–24 pixels in size.

4. Click OK, and the feather takes effect (as demonstrated in **Figure 4.11**), but it won't be noticeable on the image until you cut and paste it.

To grow a selection:

1. Create a selection using one of the selection tools.

2. Under the Selections menu, choose Grow Selection from the menu (**Selections> Modify>Grow Selection**).

3. The selection grows to encompass the adjacent areas of color to the degree tolerated by the Magic Wand tolerance settings.

✔ Tip

■ The grow command can only be applied to an image that is 24-bit color or grayscale.

To select similar color:

1. Create a selection using one of the selection tools.

2. Under the Selections menu, choose Select Similar (**Selections>Modify>Select Similar**).

3. The selection area expands out to include all the other areas of the image that have the same colors as the current selection.

To subtract areas of transparent color:

1. Create a selection using one of the selection tools.

2. Choose Transparent Color from the Selections menu , as shown in **Figure 4.12** (**Selections>Modify>Transparent Color** or Control-T). The Transparent Color Selection box appears.

3. The Transparent Color drop-down menu lets you choose which color to subtract from the selection area. The available color can be the Foreground or Background Colors, white, black, red, green, or blue. When chosen, any colors in the selected area are deselected (in effect, they become transparent when pasted down).

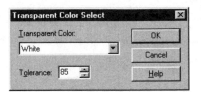

Figure 4.12 The Transparent Color Selection dialog box.

Figure 4.13 The results of subtracting the white background and shadows from the overall image selection, which produced a tight selection around the sunflower image.

✔ Tip

- If the color desired is not on the drop-down menu, you need to cancel the process and choose a new background or foreground color from within the selected area, using the Eyedropper tool.

4. Set the tolerance level. The tolerance setting is very important to the outcome of the Transparent Color modification. It determines how close the color of a given pixel has to be to the Transparent Color selected, in order for it to join the colors being dropped from the selected area.

   The tolerance level can be set anywhere from 0, meaning no tolerance (only perfect matches to the color are deselected), to 200, meaning complete tolerance (every pixel is deselected).

5. When you have your desired settings, click OK, and all color areas from within the original selection which match the transparent color (up to the set tolerance level) are removed from the selected area.

6. In **Figure 4.13**, we wanted to quickly select the basic outline of this sunflower. We decided to do it by selecting the entire image, setting the background color to white, and then subtracting white plus a decent level of tolerance (to make sure the shadows were subtracted too) from the selection. The result, shown in the figure, is a fairly tight selection of the main object.

To float and defloat a selection:

1. Float and Defloat are used when you want to copy a piece of a selection and move it within an image without disturbing the underlying image. Start by creating a selection, using one of the selection tools.

2. To float a selection (as seen in **Figure 4.14**), choose Float from the Selections menu, (**Selections>Float** or Control-F).

SELECTION OPTIONS

The image is then floating and can be moved without disturbing the underlying image.

3. To defloat a selection, go to the Selections menu, and choose Defloat (**Selections> Defloat** or Shift + Control-F). The image is pasted down in its new position.

To hide a marquee:

1. Sometimes when you're trying to precisely match up a selected area somewhere within an image, it makes sense to not have the "marching ants" or marquee blocking your view. The marquee can be hidden if desired. First, create a selection using one of the selection tools.

2. Under the Selections menu, click on Hide Marquee (**Selections>Hide Marquee** or Shift + Control-M). A check mark appears to the left of the command in the Selections menu, to denote that the selection is now hidden.

3. To show the marquee again, select Hide Marquee. The check mark disappears from the drop-down menu, and the marquee reappears.

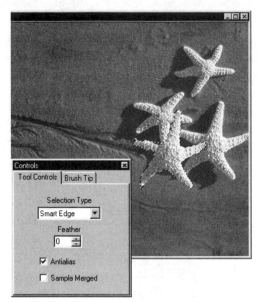

Figure 4.14 A floating selection in action.

Saving and Loading Selections

Sometimes you don't want to lose a complicated selection just because you save the image or make a new selection. Paint Shop Pro lets you save selections as their own file. Paint Shop Pro also lets you save current selections to the alpha channel of an image; with certain file formats (such as Paint Shop Pro's own format) this saves the current selection directly with an image.

This allows you to create a library of complex selections, so you don't have to recreate them every time you want to work over an area on a complex graphic. Think of it as your own personal cookie-cutter draw.

To save a selection to a file:

1. Create a selection using one of the selection tools.

2. Under the Selections menu, choose Save To Disk. The File Open/ Save As dialog box appears with Save Selection Area as its title. You can choose where it should be saved.

3. Give the file a name. The Save As type is already chosen for you.

4. Click on the Save button and the selection is saved to the area you designated.

To save a selection to an image's alpha channel:

1. Create a selection using one of the selection tools.

2. Under the Selections menu, choose Save To Alpha Channel (Selections>Save To Alpha Channel). The Save To Alpha Channel dialog box appears.

3. Make sure that the correct image is selected under Available Documents. A preview of the selection to be saved is shown. Make

sure the New Channel is highlighted under the Alpha Channel box.

4. Click OK. A New Channel box appears.

5. Select the name for the new channel, and click OK.

6. The selection is saved to the alpha channel. When you load from the alpha channel later, the name of the file you saved it as appears. **Figure 4.15** illustrates an alpha channel saved selection.

✔ Tips

■ When a selection is saved as an alpha channel, it is saved as a grayscale bitmap within the image. However, this information is retained when the image is saved to a file only if the .psp or Paint Shop Pro format is used. This image format holds the alpha channel within the image and does not discard it. TIFF and TGA files are able to hold one alpha channel; most of the other file formats do not hold any channels.

■ Even after the image is saved as an alpha channel, it still appears as a selection in the image. You can deselect it if you wish.

■ See Chapter 8 for more on alpha channels.

To load a selection from a file:

1. Activate the layer in which the selection is going to be placed.

2. Under the Selections menu, choose Load From Disk (**Selections>Load From Disk**). The File Open/Save As dialog box appears with Load Selection Area as its title. The file type will already be selected as .sel.

3. Find the file you want to load or type its name in the File Name area.

4. Click Open. The box disappears, and the selection appears on the chosen layer.

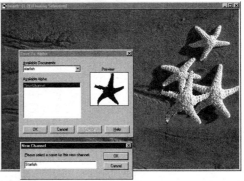

Figure 4.15 You can save selections quickly to the alpha channel of an image. The selections appear on the layers palette.

To load a selection from an alpha channel:

1. Activate the layer in which the selection is going to be placed.

2. Under the Selections menu, choose Load From Alpha Channel (**Selections>Load From Alpha Channel**). The Load From Alpha Channel box appears; it's the same box as the Save From Alpha Channel box.

3. Choose the correct selection in the Available Alpha area. The preview box displays the highlighted image.

4. When the correct selection is chosen, click OK.

5. The box disappears and the selection from the alpha channel appears in the chosen layer.

6. To delete one of the saved selections from the alpha channel, simply select Delete from the Load Alpha dialog box.

SAVING AND LOADING SELECTIONS

Working with Selections and Layers

There are two different ways to work with selections. You can move the selection within the image, or you can move only the marquee.

There are also two selection modes to use when working with a selection. The first is a floating selection, which is discussed earlier in this chapter. The floating selection becomes its own temporary layer above an image or layer. This new temporary layer can be used to modify the floating selection without altering the rest of the image. The new temporary layer is denoted by an inwardly pressed button on the layers palette which says Floating Selection on it.

The second mode is a standard selection and is part of a layer or image. When this mode of selection is moved or edited, the image is actually modified.

To move a selection within an image:

The original selection can be moved, resulting in an empty space, or a copy of the selection can be moved. Moving a copy allows the original image to remain where it was. Use the same tool to move it as you did to create the selection. The selection tool changes to the move tool when the cursor is moved across the selected area. This leaves a transparent area when complete (**Figure 4.16**).

To cut and drag a selection:

1. Start by creating a selection, using one of the selection tools.

2. Click and hold the mouse while you move the selection with the selection tool.

3. As you drag the selection, it changes into a floating selection.

Figure 4.16 When you quickly select and then drag an area of an image, you leave a transparent or background color area in the space previously occupied by the selected area.

4. Drop it where you want it to go, and remember that the selection will not be placed into a layer until it is deselected.

To copy a selection:

1. Create a selection using one of the selection tools.

2. Click and hold the Alt key while you click and hold the mouse and drag the selected area.

3. The copied selection changes to a floating selection and can be moved anywhere on the image.

4. Move and drop it where you want it to go.

5. The selection will not be placed into a new layer until it is deselected.

✔ Tips

■ To move any selection on a pixel-by-pixel basis, hold the Shift key while using the arrow keys to move the selection.

■ To move a copy the same way, Alt + click and move the selection first. Once it has been moved and the copy has been created, simply do the same as before, using the Shift key and the arrow keys. The moved selection will still change to a floating selection.

To move only the marquee:

1. Create a selection using one of the selection tools.

2. Click the Move tool on the Tools palette.

3. Right-click with the mouse on the selection, and hold the mouse button down while moving the selected area.

4. Once the selection is in the correct new position, release the mouse button.

To cut, copy and paste selections to other images:

1. Create a selection using one of the selection tools.

2. To cut a selection, leaving a hole on the original image, select Cut from the menu (**Edit>Cut** or Control-X). To copy a selection, leaving the underlying imagery intact, choose Copy from the menu (**Edit>Copy** or Control-C).

3. Once cut or copied, you can paste the image in one of five different ways

4. To paste as a new image (in which Paint Shop Pro opens a new image and places the contents from the clipboard on the new image), cut or copy your selection, and then select Paste As New Image (**Edit>Paste>As New Image**, or Control-V, or click on the Paste As New Image button on the toolbar). **Figure 4.17** shows an object selected and then pasted as a new image.

5. To paste the cut or copied selection into a new layer (**Figure 4.18**), cut or copy your selection, and then select As New Layer from the edit menu (**Edit>Paste>As New Layer** or Control-L).

6. To paste a selection from the clipboard as a new selection in any other image, cut or copy your selection (**Figure 4.19**), and then select As New Selection from the Edit menu (**Edit>Paste>As New Selection** or Control-E).

7. To paste a selection as a transparent selection into an image, cut or copy your selection and then select Paste As Transparent Selection from the menu (**Edit>Paste>As Transparent Selection** or Shift + Control-E).

8. To paste a clipped or copied selection into any other existing selection (and replace

Figure 4.17 Paste As New Image in action.

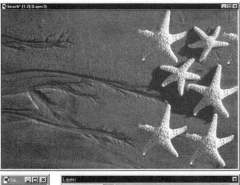
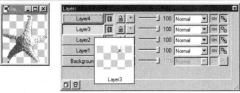

Figure 4.18 Paste As New Layer in action.

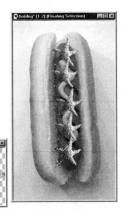

Figure 4.19 Paste As Transparent Selection in action.

the data in that current selection with the image from the clipboard), cut or copy your selection and then deselect the current selection used to make the cut or copy and create a new selection or choose an image with an existing selection. Choose Paste Into Selection from the menu (**Edit>Paste>Into Selection** or Shift Control-L).

9. Any pasted image remains as a selection until you right-click the mouse somewhere in the image to paste it down.

WORKING WITH SELECTIONS AND LAYERS

ALL ABOUT LAYERS

The Layers feature in Paint Shop Pro 5.0 is probably the single most powerful and dramatic change from previous versions of the program. Layers allow you to place portions of an image onto individual sections where they can be manipulated and changed, independent of the rest of the image. The Layers feature creates an incredible amount of control and flexibility that had previously been absent from Paint Shop Pro.

Layers Basics

Layers are individual sections on which you can place a piece of your work. Think of a layer as a piece of tracing paper. The only part you can see is where the image is — the rest of the layer is transparent, and this lets work on successive layers "shine" through. As you place the layers one on top of each other, you can see the whole picture.

The background layer is always the first one to be placed down and always remains the bottom layer. The color of the background depends on the setting selected as the background color when you create a new image. Each additional layer that is created is placed on top of the background.

If your computer has enough memory, Paint Shop Pro can support up to 64 layers in one image. You can add as many objects as you like to a given layer. The opacity for each layer can be adjusted individually. Layers can be locked or unlocked. Layers can also be deleted. The *current* layer is the specific layer that is being worked on, and you can only edit one layer at a time.

The Layers palette (**Figure 5.1**) controls most layer functionality. To select a layer, click on its name in the Layers palette. The current layer button appears pressed in, denoting that it is the layer being worked on. Make sure the appropriate layer is selected before you begin work on that layer. To view what is on a specific layer, drag the cursor towards the bottom right corner of that layer and a picture box appears (**Figure 5.2**).

Figure 5.1 The Layers palette.

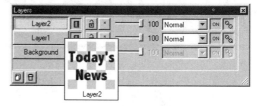

Figure 5.2 To quickly see what imagery is contained in a specific layer, hold the mouse pointer over the layer name.

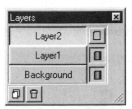

Figure 5.3 Click on the Layer Visibility toggle button to turn visibility of a layer on or off.

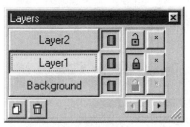

Figure 5.4 A small lock next to a layer means it is locked.

Figure 5.5 You can quickly promote a background into a layer by choosing Promote to Layer from this menu.

The Layers Palette

The Layers palette opens when the program opens and should remain on the desktop when the document is being worked on. You use the Layers palette to create new layers and edit specific parts of your design. If the Layers palette is not visible, click on the Layers button on the toolbar or choose **Layers>View**.

To work with the Layers palette:

1. The first button on the Layers palette contains the Layer Name. Click on the layer name to be worked on.

2. Next to the layer name is the Layer Visibility toggle (see **Figure 5.3**). The button has a multicolor square on it. The appearance of the colors indicates that the corresponding layer is part of the visible view. Click on the square to make the layer invisible, and the square's colors disappear to reflect that setting.

3. Next to the Layer Visibility toggle is the Protect Transparency toggle (**Figure 5.4**), used to lock and unlock specific layers individually.

   Protecting allows you to edit only the pixels contained in an image. It does not allow you to continue adding to the transparent part of that layer. This is useful when you want to preserve the transparent selection but edit the existing image.

   When a layer is unlocked, the padlock is green and looks unlocked. When you click on the Protect Transparency toggle, it locks and turns red. Before you can edit the transparent section, it must be unlocked.

   The background layer cannot be locked or unlocked unless it is *promoted* to a layer. This is done by right-clicking on the layer name or the Layer Visibility toggle and selecting Promote to Layer (**Figure 5.5**).

4. To the right of the Protect Transparency toggle is the Layer Group toggle. Use Layer Group to group one layer with another layer or add a layer to an existing group.

When the layer is ungrouped, an asterisk is visible. Click on the toggle to group the layer. A number appears in place of the asterisk. The first number will be 1. Then choose the next layer to be grouped with it; the same number will appear next to this layer where the asterisk once was. To group another set of layers, simply click on the button with a 1 on it, and this button changes to a 2. Click again, and it becomes a 3, and so on. To pair up layers, continue clicking on the button until their numbers match.

5. Next to the Layer Group toggle is the Layer Opacity slider. Layer opacity ranges from 0–100 percent. Opacity allows an underlying layer to show through and makes the layer on top of the image appear darker and more prominent. A layer doesn't have to be current to change its opacity; just move any of the sliders associated with that layer.

When changing the opacity of a layer, all the image information stays the same. Changing opacity just makes the image appear universally more transparent or more solid. The higher the percentage number, the more solid the image. The farther you move the Layer Opacity slider to the left, the lighter and more transparent the image becomes (see **Figure 5.6**).

An opacity of 0 means the image on that layer is 100-percent transparent.

✔ Tip

■ It is good to have all the layers viewable when working with the opacity so that you can judge the total effect on the image as you adjust each individual layer's opacity.

Figure 5.6 The effect when you slide a layer's opacity down, making this text increasingly more transparent.

Original

More transparent

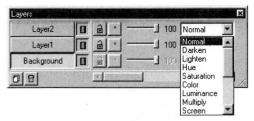

Figure 5.7 The Blend Mode pull-down menu.

6. The next option on the Layers palette is the Layers Blend Mode pull-down menu (See **Figure 5.7**). There are seventeen additional blend modes. When you choose a blend mode, the blend is previewed on the image (you are not permanently setting the blend mode at this moment). The blend affects all layers, not just the one directly underneath it. To permanently apply a desired blend mode, you must merge the layers together. For more on this, see the "Understanding Blend Modes" sidebar.

7. The Enable Layer Mask toggle is next. The default is "on." When on, the layer can be seen with the selected mask. Off makes the mask non-viewable. Clicking on the button toggles the setting. This button controls the appearance of the layer.

8. The last button on the Layers palette is the Link Mask toggle, used to move the mask and combine it with a layer. The default is On. When on, the Flip, Rotate, and Mirror commands move the mask and the layer together. Off means the mask will be separated from the layer.

9. Located on the bottom left corner of the palette is the Add New Layer button, which lets you add layers. Clicking on the Add New Layer Button causes the Layer Properties box to appear. To the right is the Delete Layer button, which is used to delete a layer.

THE LAYERS PALETTE

75

The Layers Properties Dialog Box

The Layers Properties dialog box appears when you create a new layer or set the options. At any point, you can set properties by double-clicking on a specific layer; the Layers Properties dialog box appears (**Figure 5.8**). Or you select Layers>Properties.

To set properties of layers:

Layers are automatically named in numerical order (layer 1, layer 2, and so on). To name the layer, change it in the Name box. The next group of options can be set right from the Layers palette. The Layers Properties box is just another place to set or change them.

The difference between the Layers Properties dialog box and the Layers palette is the inclusion of Blend Ranges. The Blend Ranges option allows you to set the specific range of colors that are affected by blend modes. You can set the constraints of Blend by brightness or channel value.

In the Blend Ranges panel, select the channel Blend should use to compare with layers during blend mode: Gray, Red, Green, or Blue. The Gray channel is for when you want the blend range to depend on the lightness value.

Sliding the arrows across the *opacity ramp* lets you set the constraints. The top group of arrows sets the highest opacity level, and the bottom sets the lowest level. The opacity can range from 0 - 100 percent.

When you are done setting the properties for a layer, click OK to return to image editing.

✔ Tip

■ You can use the double-click option and rename a layer at any time.

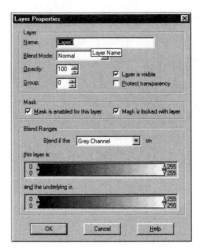

Figure 5.8 The Layers Properties dialog box.

Working with Layers

Now that you have an understanding of what the Layers palette is and how it works, let's put this knowledge to use.

To create a new layer:

1. Click on the Add New Layer button on the Layers palette or choose **Layers>New**.

2. The Layers Properties dialog box appears. Fill in the information you want and click OK at the bottom of the page. Your new layer appears in the Layers palette.

To turn selections into layers:

1. Create a new layer or choose the layer on which the new image will be placed.

2. Create type or any other floating selection.

3. After placing the text or image in the appropriate place, right-click on the image to deselect it. The image is automatically placed on the layer created in step 1. If you don't select a layer before creating the image, it defaults to the last layer selected.

To hide or show a layer:

1. Select a layer.

2. Click the Layer Visibility toggle on the Layers palette next to the layer you want to eliminate from view. Or double-click the layer to be hidden. The Layers Properties box appears. Click on the check mark next to the Visibility toggle and click OK. The layer is then hidden.

3. To show the layer, click the Visibility toggle again. Any time you select a layer it returns to view. Or right-click on the Layer palette and choose **View>Current Only or All**. This option can also be found in the Layers drop-down menu and allows you to view the desired layer or all of them.

WORKING WITH LAYERS

The order in which the layers are set is not carved in stone. Layers can be placed in any order to suit your needs as you progress.

To arrange layers:

1. To move a layer to a new position, click and hold the layer buttons to be moved. Drag the layer up or down. A hand icon appears when the layer is moved.

2. To place a layer above another layer, move the hand cursor so it is slightly above the layer you want to be beneath and release the mouse button. To place a layer below another layer, position the hand cursor so it is slightly below the layer you want to be beneath and release the mouse button.

   Another way to restack layers is to click the layer to be moved and choose **Layers> Arrange.** You can choose to bring the layer to the Top, Move Up, Move Down, or Send to Bottom. Pick one, and that action takes place.

✔ Tip

■ It is useful to lock a layer when you want to preserve its transparency. Locking assures that when you are editing on a locked layer, only the pixels that are present will be changed. The work performed on a locked layer only occurs on the image in the layer — not on the empty space around the image.

To lock and unlock layers:

1. To lock, click the Protect Transparency toggle on the Layers palette or choose Protect Transparency in the Layers Properties dialog box.

2. To unlock, simply click the button again or uncheck the box in the Layers Properties dialog box.

To delete a layer:

1. Select the layer to be deleted.

2. Drag the layer on top of the Delete Layer button on the Layers palette and release the mouse button. A dialog box appears, asking whether you are sure you want to delete this layer — if you are, click OK.

   Another method is to select a layer and click on the Delete Layer button. A confirmation dialog box appears. Click OK if you are sure you want to delete the layer.

Grouping, Merging, and Flattening Layers

Grouping specific layers allows you to apply the same effects to multiple layers, without having to merge them together or run the same filters and processes on each layer individually. *Merging* allows you to combine two or more layers into a single layer. *Flattening* places all the layers into one layer. The difference is that merging merges only layers that are set to visible into one layer, and flattening merges *all* layers, regardless of visibility, into a single one-layer image.

Remember that merging or flattening layers causes the blend modes selected for the layers to take effect.

To group layers:

1. Select a layer to be grouped.

2. Click on the Layer Group toggle or go to the Layers Properties box and choose the number for Group (**Figure 5.9**). Assign the same number to the layers you want grouped together.

To merge layers:

1. Make visible all the layers to be merged.

2. Make invisible any layers you want to remain as individual layers.

3. Choose Layers>Merge>Merge Visible. This combines the layers that you have selected as visible layers.

Flattening an image quickly combines all layers into a single layer.

To flatten an image:

1. Choose Layers>Merge>Merge All.

2. All the layers are combined into one.

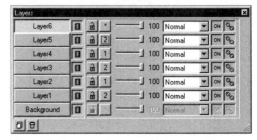

Figure 5.9 Preparing Layers to be group.

✔ Tip

■ Any time you save a multilayer image to a file format that doesn't support multi-layers, your image is automatically flattened.

Understanding Blend Modes

To see these modes illustrated, check out this book's Color Section.

Normal: Pixels on the current layer are blended with the layer underneath only by varying the opacity.

Darken: Pixels in the selected layer, which are darker than the pixels in the layer below, are applied to the image. Pixels lighter than the layers underneath disappear.

Lighten: Blend and base colors that are lighter will be displayed.

Hue: The hue of layers underneath will be applied to the selected layer.

Saturation: The saturation of selected layers will be applied to layers below.

Color: Although the luminance of layers below the selected layer will be affected, this blend mode applies both the hue and saturation of the selected layer to layers underneath.

Luminance: The luminance of the selected layer is applied to layers underneath, leaving the color unaffected.

Multiply: The colors of the selected layer are combined with the layers underneath it to produce a darker color. Any color that is multiplied by a black color remains black, whereas any color multiplied by white is left unchanged. This blend mode produces the same results no matter which layer is on top.

Screen: Lightens the underlying layer's color. This mode produces the same results no matter which layer is on top.

Dissolve: Replaces the colors of some pixels on the selected layer randomly with those of the layers below to create a speckled or noise-style effect. The layer's opacity determines the extent of the number of pixels replaced.

Overlay: Applies one of two blend modes to layers. If the color channel value of the underlying layers is less than one-half of the maximum value, it applies the Multiply blend to the layer. If the color channel value is greater than or equal to half, it applies the Screen blend mode. The result: lighter colors are exposed to the Screen blend mode, whereas the Multiply blend mode is applied to darker colors, which tends to keep shadows and highlights of layers below intact.

Hard Light: Similar to Overlay blend mode. If the selected layer's color channel value is less than 128 (half the maximum value), it uses the Multiply blend mode. If the value is greater than or equal to 128, it uses the Screen blend mode.

Soft Light: Combines the two previous blend modes. If the selected layer's color channel value is less than half the maximum value, the Burn mode is used. If the it is greater than or equal to half, the Dodge blend mode is used. This mode is generally used to add soft highlights or shadows.

Difference: The color of the selected layer's pixels is subtracted from those of the underlying layers if it is lighter. This mode produces the same results no matter which layer is on top.

Dodge: Lightens the underlying layers, using the selected layer's lightness values. Light colors produce the most lightening, whereas black and darker colors have little or no effect.

Burn: The lightness values of the colors of the blend layer reduce the lightness of the underlying layers, darkening the image.

Exclusion: Works in a similar fashion to the Difference blend mode but with a softer effect.

ALL ABOUT COLOR

If there is one aspect of computer graphics creation that separates those who are truly experienced from those who aren't, it's probably color. Paint Shop Pro contains a number of tools that give you excellent control over the color of your imagery. In particular, it offers terrific features and processes for creating images with a limited number of colors that reduce file size for faster Web delivery and still leave your images looking great.

Color Basics

The foundation of computer graphics is called a *pixel*, which is short for picture element. A pixel is one point on a graphical image. Thus, when we say an image has a resolution of 320 x 200, we are saying that it measures 320 pixels across and 200 down. By multiplying, we find that 320 x 200 image contains 64,000 pixels.

Pixels essentially are points of light presented on the monitor's screen. Depending on your computer system and the resolution of your screen, you can have a screen display that measures anywhere from 640 x 480 pixels up to 1280 x 1152 or higher.

Because pixels are displayed on monitors, their color is composed of light. A precise mixture of light, in three distinct colors of red, green, and blue (RGB), determines the color of each pixel. If you set all three RGB colors to their highest settings, they produce white pixels. At their lowest settings, they produce black. When set individually to any number of different levels, they can produce an entire spectrum of colors.

The RGB color scheme just described is what is known as a *color model*. RGB is just one of several color models used in computer graphics and other graphic arts arenas. Two other color models you'll run into are HSL (Hue, Saturation, Luminance) and CMYK (Cyan, Magenta, Yellow, Black).

Two other color models you may sometimes hear about are CIE/LAB, a color model used in Europe, and Pantone, which is a high-end color system used by professional printers and graphic artists. Paint Shop Pro does not support CIE/LAB or Pantone color systems. It does add support for Hexadecimal color, which is nothing more than a different way of referencing RGB color codes. Hexadecimal codes are used in HTML tags to specify colors in Web pages.

Another important aspect of color is something known as *bit-depth*, which is sometimes referred to as *bit-planes*. Bit-depth refers to how many colors an image (or graphics card) can support. Essentially, the number of colors an image can support is 2n colors with n being the number of bits per pixel at which it is set. For example, a 4-bit image (an image with a 4-bit depth) can support 16 colors (2^4 is 16). Most images you see are either 8-, 16-, or 24-bit images. So, 8-bit color means 256 colors; 16-bit color means 65,536 colors; and 24-bit color means 16,777,216 colors.

✔ Tip

- Sometimes you hear about 15-bit color, which supports 32,268 colors. This is because a number of graphics cards support up to 15-bit color but not 16-bit color.

When creating images that support 16 million colors, the RGB color model offers you the chance to set each element to one of 256 levels or shades. Also, even if your system doesn't support 16 million colors, you can still paint in that mode – you just won't be able to see the purest presentation. Instead, your graphics card will approximate the color and display the nearest color it can. Because most people run their computers at a color depth of 16-bit or better, you should notice little difference.

You can adjust three main elements in an image's color scheme: light and dark, hue and saturation, and bit-depth and palette adjustment.

Let's go through each color feature step by step and then look at some common color adjustment situations and how to handle them.

Light and Dark Adjustments

Adjustments concerning how light or dark an image or portions of an image will be very important to the overall quality of the image, especially with scans and other photo-realistic imagery.

✔ Tip

■ Light and dark includes not only the overall brightness of an image, but other levels of light and dark, including shadows and midtone coloring. In many cases, light and dark adjustments do more to clear up and sharpen an image than any other color process.

To adjust brightness/contrast:

1. Choose the image or make a selection where you want to change the brightness and/or contrast.

2. Choose **Colors>Adjust>Brightness/Contrast** or press Shift-B. The Brightness/Contrast dialog box appears (**Figure 6.1**).

3. The sliders control the settings, which can be positive (+100%), negative (-100%), or neutral (0). Set the sliders to the desired settings. When you've found the setting you want, click OK or press Enter.

To adjust highlights/midtones/shadows:

1. Chose the image or make a selection where you want to change the highlights/midtones/shadows.

2. Choose **Colors>Adjust>Highlights/Midtones/Shadows** or press Shift-M.

3. The Highlights/Midtones/Shadows dialog box appears (**Figure 6.2**).

4. The sliders control the settings, which can be set from 0 to 100. The settings initially

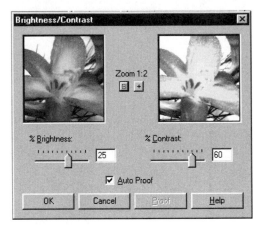

Figure 6.1 The Brightness/Contrast dialog box.

Figure 6.2 The Highlights/Midtones/Shadows dialog box.

open with Highlights set to 100, Midtones set to 50, and Shadows set to 0.

Each slider has a slightly different effect on the image. The Highlights slider adds lightness as it moves to the left — it lightens increasingly darker pixels, which adds more brightness and highlights.

The Midtones slider lightens midtone areas of the image as the slider moves right, and darkens midtone areas as it moves left.

The Shadows slider does the opposite of the Highlights slider: As you move it to the right, it removes lightness proportionally from the image, increasingly darkening lighter pixels.

5. When you've found the settings you want, click OK or press Enter.

To make an image grayscale:

1. Select the image you want to turn to grayscale.

2. Choose **Colors>Grayscale**.

Histogram Functions

The *histogram* is essentially how color is distributed throughout an image. You can view the current histogram by viewing the Histogram tool (**Figure 6.3**), which graphs the amount of RGB in the image. By varying how various levels of color are in an image you can further adjust the color makeup of an image.

There are several types of histogram functions:

Equalizing an image creates a total balance between light and dark areas on an image. Equalizing tends to be most useful when working with photos taken outside on hazy days. Be careful—look what it did to the clouds (**Figure 6.4**).

Stretching an image pushes up the contrast of the image, so that all possible values are used. When it works well, it tends to improve the sharpness of the picture (**Figure 6.5**).

You can also individually adjust hues using the Hue Map function, improve the gamma of the image, as well as individually add or subtract the amount of red, green or blue in your image.

To equalize an image:

1. Chose the image or selection area you want to equalize.

2. Chose Colors>Histogram Functions>Equalize or press Shift-E.

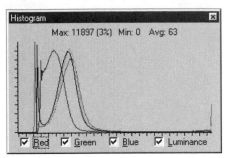

Figure 6.3 The Histogram tool.

Figure 6.4 Before and after examples of Equalize.

Before

After

HISTOGRAM FUNCTIONS

Figure 6.5 Before and after example of Stretch.

Before

After

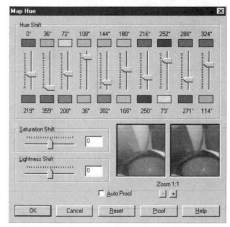

Figure 6.6 The Hue Map dialog box.

To stretch an image:

1. Chose the image or selection area you want to stretch.

2. Chose **Colors>Histogram Functions >Stretch** or press Shift-T.

To adjust the Hue Map:

1. Choose the image or selection area you want to adjust.

2. Choose **Colors>Adjust>Hue Map**. The Hue Map dialog box appears (**Figure 6.6**).

3. The Hue Map works like a graphic equalizer on a stereo, except it adjusts the hue of different colors in an image or selection.

   To adjust the hue, look at the sliders presented. Each is set to control a different color; as you slide that particular hue's slider, it changes color. As a result, pixels of that color or very near to it also change their hue to the adjusted color. If a hue is not represented in the image, nothing happens.

✔ Tip

- Click the Reset button to return the sliders to their default positions.

4. Use the Saturation slider to decrease the overall saturation in the image or selection area. At 100, the image becomes a grayscale image.

5. Use the Lightness slider to increase and decrease the lightness in the image. When set to -100%, the image or selection area is pure black. +100 produces pure white.

6. Once you have the desired setting, click OK or press Enter.

To adjust Gamma Correction:

1. Choose **Colors>Adjust>Gamma Correction**. The Gamma Correction dialog box appears (**Figure 6.7**). It consists of before and after preview boxes; three sliders for adjusting the red, green, and blue gamma; and a graph that shows the shape of the resulting gamma curve.

2. The default setting is for all the sliders to be linked. That means all the settings of the sliders are equal. To unlink the sliders, uncheck the link checkbox located below the sliders.

3. To set a slider, slide it back and forth or type a setting directly into the associated text box. The maximum value is 5.00, the minimum is .20, and you may enter any number in .01 intervals.

4. To lighten the colors by increasing the gamma, move the sliders to the right or increase the value to above 1.00.

5. To darken the colors by decreasing the gamma in the image, move the sliders to the right or decrease the value to below 1.00.

6. When you are satisfied with the results (**Figure 6.8**), choose OK.

To adjust Red/Green/Blue levels:

1. Choose **Colors>Adjust>Red/Green/Blue**.

2. The Red/Green/Blue dialog box appears (**Figure 6.9**). It contains a before and after preview box and three sliders for increasing or decreasing the level of Red, Green, or Blue.

3. The midpoint setting for each level is 0. At that point the level remains unchanged in the image. Slide the levels to the left to subtract more of that color from the image. Slide the levels to the right to increase more of that color in the image.

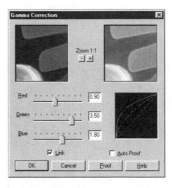

Figure 6.7
The Gamma Correction dialog box.

Figure 6.8 Before and after example of the gamma correction process where we lightened the image by moving the gamma up a bit.

Before

After

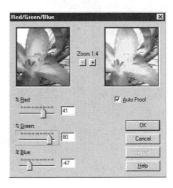

Figure 6.9 The Red/Green/Blue dialog box.

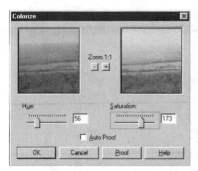

Figure 6.10 The Colorize dialog box.

Figure 6.11 Before and after negative.

Before

After

You may also type values into the associated boxes for each slider. The maximum value is 100, and the minimum value is -100.

4. When you are satisfied with the results, click OK or press Enter.

✔ Tip

■ Red/Green/Blue levels are best used to remove patches of discoloration, such as red eye. One feature common to many digital cameras is the tendency toward light bands of redness around the edges of a photograph. Sometimes increasing the Green and Blue levels instead of subtracting Red works even better.

To colorize an image:

1. Choose the image or selection area you want to colorize.

2. Choose **Colors>Colorize** or press Shift-L. The Colorize dialog box appears (**Figure 6.10**)

3. Set the Hue you want and then set the Saturation, using the sliders. Or type in the desired value instead.

4. When you find the setting you want, click OK or press Enter.

To create a negative:

1. Choose the image or selection area you want.

2. Choose **Colors>Negative**. The image or selection changes to a negative (**Figure 6.11**)

HISTOGRAM FUNCTIONS

Bit-Depth and Palette Adjustment

Bit-depth and palette adjustments are used to directly change and adjust the number of colors in an image (add or reduce). When your image is set to 256 colors or less, you can design the colors for each specific entry in the palette — a rarely needed but sometimes very useful feature.

Posterizing is used to reduce the number of colors in an image by reducing the bit-depth of each color channel. As we mentioned earlier, the fewer bits per channel, the fewer colors in the image.

To posterize an image:

1. Choose the image you want or make a selection on a section of an image.

2. Choose **Colors>Posterize** or press Shift-Z.

3. The Posterize dialog box appears (**Figure 6.12**). Choose the number of Bits Per Channel from 1 to 7 by sliding the scale.

4. Slide the slider to the left to reduce the number of bits per channel. As the bits per channel decrease, less gradation appears between colors in the image, as larger areas of single color develop.

5. Once you have the desired setting, click OK or press Enter. See **Figure 6.13** for an example of posterization.

✔ Tip

■ When reducing the colors in an image, posterizing can provide some interesting and useful results. Remember, though, that after posterizing an image, you still need to reduce the overall bit-depth.

Solarize is similar to negative, except you can control the threshold at which that colors in the image invert to the negative lightness value.

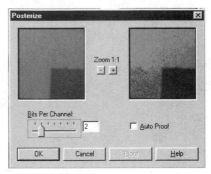

Figure 6.12 The Posterize dialog box.

Figure 6.13 Before and after posterizing.

Before

After

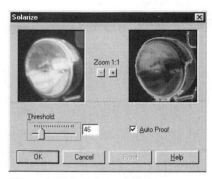

Figure 6.14 The Solarize dialog box.

Figure 6.15 Before and after solarize.

Before

After

To solarize an image:

1. Choose the image or selection area desired.

2. Choose **Colors>Solarize**.

3. The Solarize dialog box appears (**Figure 6.14**). You can choose the threshold setting at which point pixels above the threshold flip to their negative color.

4. Once you have the desired setting, click OK or press Enter. See **Figure 6.15** for a before and after example of the Solarize process.

To begin editing a palette, you need to make sure you are working with an image that has 256 or fewer colors. If your image has more than 256 colors, use color reduction to set it to 256 colors.

To edit a palette:

1. Choose **Colors>Edit Palette**, or Shift-P. The Edit Palette dialog box appears (**Figure 6.16**).

2. The Sort Order drop-down list lets you reorganize the entries according to Palette Order, Luminance, or Hue.

3. To actually change a color, choose an entry and double-click on it. This brings up the Color Picking dialog box. Choose the color to which you want to change the palette entry and click OK or press Enter. The palette entry changes to that color.

✔ Tips

- You can choose to save (**Colors>Save Palette**) and load (**Colors>Load Palette** or press Shift-O) 256-color palettes. This is useful if you want to apply the same exact palette to a number of images, or if you have a specific palette you like to start with when creating 256-color images.

- Palettes are saved to their own file (.pal files) using standard Windows dialog boxes.

To determine the number of colors in an image:

1. Choose the picture and layer for which you want to determine the color count.

2. Choose **Colors>Count Colors Used**.

3. When the answer dialog box is displayed (**Figure 6.17**), click OK or press Enter to return to editing.

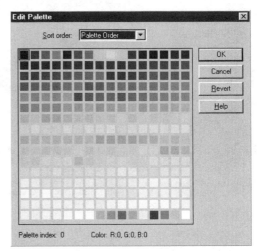

Figure 6.16 The Edit Palette dialog box.

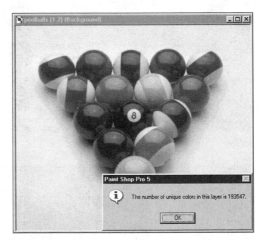

Figure 6.17 The Color Count dialog box.

BIT-DEPTH AND PALETTE ADJUSTMENT

PAINTING AND DRAWING

In order to create beautiful images with Paint Shop Pro, you have to know how to use the painting and drawing tools.

In this chapter, we explain the ins and outs of these tools, as well as some color features that go along with them.

Some Basics

Make sure the toolbar is on the screen. To show or hide the toolbar, select **View>Toolbars**. The Toolbars dialog box appears. Select the palettes and bars you want to appear on the screen.

✔ Tip

■ Most of the tools can only operate or give a desired effect if the image is at least 24-bit color or grayscale. You may need to increase the color depth (see Chapter 6) before you begin with these tools or you'll get an error like that shown in **Figure 7.1**.

Before using any of these tools, you may want to choose a color. The right-hand side of the screen has the color palette (**Figure 7.2**). When the cursor is dragged over the multiple color palette, it turns into the eyedropper. By clicking on a color section with the eyedropper, you select a color. The primary mouse button selects the foreground color, and the right mouse button selects the background.

Under the multicolor palette are two boxes filled with color: The top left box is foreground; lower right background. To switch them, click on the arrows next to the boxes. Below all the boxes is the current color information box. When you drag the cursor (which turns into the eyedropper) over the color palette, the colors under it appear in this box. To select a color, click when a desired color appears in the box. That color will appear in the appropriate color box. Another way to choose a color is by clicking on either the foreground or background color box. This opens the color dialog box (**Figure 7.3**).

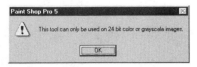

Figure 7.1 Many drawing tools discussed in this chapter require you to work in 16 million-color mode.

Figure 7.2 The color palette found usually on the right-hand side of your screen.

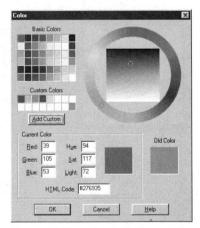

Figure 7.3 The color dialog box used in Paint Shop Pro 5 is a little different than the standard Windows color dialog box.

Figure 7.4 The first tab in the Paintbrush control panel lets you set the paper texture.

Figure 7.5 The Brush Tip control panel lets you create a million different types of brushes.

Basic Drawing Tools

Paint Shop Pro includes a number of drawing tools. Three of the most often used are the basic paintbrush, the airbrush, and the eraser.

To use the Paintbrush tool:

1. Open a new or old image.

2. Select the Paintbrush tool on the toolbar. The Paintbrush control panel appears (if not, press the letter O). It has two tabs. The first (**Figure 7.4**) controls the paper texture (more on this later). Click on the Brush Tip tab to select the option for this tool (**Figure 7.5**).

4. The top-most box on the left side shows you what the brush tip looks like. As you change the options, the brush tip changes. Notice the ratio the brush is shown in; 1:1 indicates shows it at the size it will print at.

5. Under the Shape drop-down box, you can choose the shape you want the brush to be. The choices are round, square, vertical, horizontal, right slash, and left slash.

6. The button with the paintbrush-tip icon on it, next to the Shape option, gives you drawing implement options. You can choose paintbrush, pen, pencil, marker, crayon, chalk, charcoal, or custom, which is discussed later in the chapter under Brush Tips and Custom Brushes from Images. When you select one of these options, the paintbrush draws lines that resemble drawing on a piece of paper with that particular medium.

7. With the Size slider, choose the size of the brush in pixels.

8. The Opacity slider allows you to choose the solidity of the line. At 100 percent, the line is a solid color. The lower the opacity, the lighter and more faded the

line looks. **Figure 7.6** shows several lines drawn with the brush set to higher levels of opacity.

9. Change the brush edges with the Hardness slider. At 100 percent, the edges are solid. As the hardness decreases, edges become fuzzier. **Figure 7.7** shows various lines drawn with increasing levels of hardness.

10. The Density slider changes the amount of color applied to the image with the brush. If the Density is 100 percent, the painted line is almost solid, depending on the brush chosen. As the Density lessens, the line becomes more speckled and less solid. **Figure 7.8** shows various lines drawn with increasing levels of density.

11. The Step slider controls the size of the brush step. It controls the spacing between the drops of paint or how often the brush tip touches the image during a stroke. The number represents a percentage of the brush tip's diameter. As the number decreases, the brush tip touches the image more often. The outline becomes less noticeable and the strokes appear smoother and more dense. See **Figure 7.9**.

   Once you have chosen all the options you want, you can begin painting.

12. Click and hold the mouse button while you drag the mouse over the image area. With the primary mouse button, you draw with the foreground color; the right mouse button lets you draw with the background. When you are finished drawing, release the mouse, and the line will be drawn.

13. Hold Shift while clicking with the Paintbrush tool to paint a straight line. Click where you want the line to begin, and where you want it to end. From one click to the next, a straight line is created.

Figure 7.6 You can vary the opacity of a brush stroke using the opacity option on the Brush Tip control panel.

Figure 7.7 You can vary the hardness of a brush strokes using the Hardness slider on the Brush Tip control panel.

Figure 7.8 Vary the density of a brush stroke using the Density slider on the Brush tip control panel.

BASIC DRAWING TOOLS

Figure 7.9 Vary the spacing between strokes by using the Step setting on the Brush Tip control panel.

Figure 7.10 The Airbrush tool puts down more paint the longer you hold it over the same area.

To use the Airbrush tool:

1. Open a new or old image.

2. Select the Airbrush tool from the toolbar.

3. The Airbrush tool works exactly like the Paintbrush tool, and has all the same features and control panel options (see earlier in this chapter).

4. The difference between the Airbrush and Paintbrush tools is that the Airbrush closely resembles the effect of an airbrush or spray paint. Even with the same numbers inserted on both tools for the brush tips, the Airbrush tool's edges are fuzzier. **Figure 7.10** shows the Airbrush tool in action.

5. To draw a straight line with the Airbrush tool, see steps 12 and 13 for the Paintbrush tool previously in this chapter.

To use the Eraser tool:

1. Open a new or existing image. Use the Eraser tool to erase sections of an image or canvas. Erasing with the primary mouse button leaves the background color visible; the right button leaves the foreground color visible (note that this is opposite of how the Paintbrush and Airbrush tools work).

2. Select the Eraser tool on the toolbar. The control panel appears (if not, press the letter O).

3. Set the Paper Texture in the Tool Controls tab (more on this later in this chapter). You can also set Brush Tip options on the Brush Tip tab.

4. If you make a mistake and want to fix it, choose the appropriate color for the foreground or background and erase the correct section using the appropriate mouse button.

BASIC DRAWING TOOLS

5. After you select the Eraser tool from the toolbar and choose all the options you want, click and drag the mouse along the canvas. Release the mouse button when you have completed the line. Repeat these steps to draw as many lines as desired.

✔ Tips

■ To draw a straight line with the Eraser tool, hold Shift while clicking where you want the line to begin. Click again where you want it to end. Between the two points, a straight line is drawn. When finished drawing, release the Shift key.

■ The Opacity slider determines how dark or light the line is drawn. At 100 percent opacity, a solid line is created; at 0 percent, the line is virtually imperceptible.

Figure 7.11 You can draw straight or bezier curved lines.

Figure 7.12 The Line tool in action.

Lines and Shapes

If you're someone who has a problem drawing a straight line even with a ruler or a circle with a compass, you should love computer drawing programs like Paint Shop Pro. Included in the basic drawing tools are automated lines, circles, ovals, squares, and rectangles.

To draw lines:

1. Select the Line tool. The control panel appears (if it does not, press the letter O). This tool does not use the Brush Tip settings, only the Tool Controls settings.

2. On the Tool Control Panel (**Figure 7.11**), select a line type: Normal or Bezier. Normal allows you to draw a straight line. With Bezier, you first draw a line and then you may move it twice thereafter, in order to mold it into a dynamically curved line.

3. You can also use the spin control to set the width of the line in pixels.

4. To make the lines smoother, put a check in the Antialias checkbox.

5. When the Line tool is selected, and the cursor is dragged over the image, the cursor turns into cross hairs. To draw a straight line, place the cross hairs at the starting point of the line. Click and drag (primary mouse button uses foreground color, right mouse button uses background color), drawing a straight line between these two points.

6. Release the mouse button. A line with correct width and color is created. **Figure 7.12** shows a number of straight lines drawn using the line tool.

✔ Tip

■ To create a line in 45-degree increments hold down Shift during steps 5 and 6.

LINES AND SHAPES

7. If you are drawing a Bezier line, click on the line again and while holding down the right mouse button drag away in any given direction. This creates a semicircle curve.

8. To create an S-shaped curve, drag the line again in the opposite direction. **Figure 7.13** shows a number of curved lines drawn using the Bezier curve option.

To draw specific shapes:

1. Choose the colors you want to use.

2. Select the Shape tool. The control panel should appear (if not, press the letter O). On the control panel (see **Figure 7.14**) only the Tool Controls section is relevant.

3. On the Tool Controls, select the shape you want: Rectangle, Square, Ellipse, or Circle.

4. Select a Style, either Filled or Outlined. Use the spin control to set the Outline Width. The width of the shape's boundaries will be set in pixels.

5. To make the edges appear smoother, click on the Antialias checkbox. With all the options set, you can now use the tool. Select the colors you want to use.

6. Drag the cursor over the image, and it turns into cross hairs. Place the cross hairs at the beginning point of the rectangle or square. Click and hold while you drag it in the direction you want the shape to go.

For a circle or ellipse, the cross hairs emanate from the center of the shapes. When you move the cursor, the circle or ellipse grows both ways. The starting point ends up being the middle of the shape.

7. Release the mouse button when the shape is completed. The filled or outlined shape then appears. **Figure 7.15** shows a variety of shapes drawn using the shape tool.

Figure 7.13 Drawing elegant curves is a snap with the Bezier curve tool.

Figure 7.14 The Shape tool control panel.

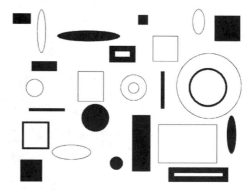

Figure 7.15 Perfect circles, squares, ovals, and rectangles in seconds.

Figure 7.16 The Color Replacer control tab.

Color Replacement

The Color Replacer tool replaces one color with another from the same image. It is especially useful when the color you are changing isn't grouped in an area in which you could easily use the fill tool.

To use the Color Replacer tool:

1. Open an existing image in which you would like to have a color replaced.

2. Click the Color Replacer tool on the toolbar. The control panel appears (if not, press the letter O).

3. Click on the Tool Control tab (**Figure 7.16**). Here you can adjust the Tolerance setting. Tolerance determines how close the color must be for it to be replaced.

   The settings range from 0 to 200. A setting of 0 means that there is no tolerance, and the color would have to be a perfect match in order to be replaced. 200 means total tolerance — all the colors will be replaced whether they match the color or not. 100 is halfway and replaces most of the chosen color, along with some other colors that contain the chosen color. For example, if you are replacing yellow with purple, all of the yellow will be replaced, along with some orange and other colors that are close to yellow in the RGB color model.

4. The Brush Tip tab allows you to set the brush tip size. Click it to adjust the options (options are explained in the Paintbrush section earlier in this chapter).

5. Choose the color you want to replace with the eyedropper. Click on the eyedropper on the toolbar and select the foreground color with the primary mouse button and the background color with the right.

COLOR REPLACEMENT

As you drag over the image, the color you can select appears in the bottom-most box related to the color picker. Or choose the color from the multicolor section.

6. Once you have a foreground and background color, select Color Replacer. The settings you last chose will still be there.

7. You can replace all the foreground color with the background color, or vice versa. The Color Replacer changes all the background when you double-click with the primary mouse button; the foreground changes with the right mouse button.

8. To replace color in a specific area, select it beforehand using one of the selection tools. The color is only affected in the selected area. If the colors you want to change are on a specific layer, make sure that layer is the active layer. Color replacement only occurs in the current layer.

   The Color Replacer tool swaps background and foreground colors depending on which button you use. Select the tool, click and hold on an area, and drag in the direction you want it to go. The only place a line appears is where the color goes over the foreground or background color.

9. When you click and hold the primary mouse button while you drag over green color, it replaces green with yellow. The opposite happens if you click, hold, and drag the right mouse button. The yellow changes to green when the cursor is dragged over yellow. **Figure 7.17** shows replacement of lighter inner areas of a flower with a darker color.

10. To end a line, release the mouse button.

✔ Tip

■ For a straight line, hold Shift while clicking on the beginning and ending points.

Figure 7.17 The Color Replacer Tool in action.

Figure 7.18 Use the Tool Controls to change the retouch mode.

Retouching and Textures

If you would like to retouch your image using filter-like effects, use the Retouch tool. It gives you pixel-by-pixel hand control over the application of most filter effects and some color effects. For more, see Chapters 6 and 9.

Another neat effect for your retouching and painting efforts is to set the texture of the paper you're drawing on. If you want to simulate working on canvas or bricks, Paint Shop Pro 5 lets you set the canvas to simulate that texture.

To use the Retouch tool:

1. Open the image you want to retouch and select the Retouch tool. The control panel appears (if not, press the letter O).

2. Click on the Brush Tips tab to choose the brush tip options you want.

   Click on the Tool Controls tab to select a Retouch Mode (**Figure 7.18**). Some of the modes contain the same effects as those in **Color>Adjust Color**. Other Retouch Modes have the same effects as those in **Image>Filter**. These modes determine which effect applies to the image, and brush tips determine how they are applied.

3. Using the Tool Controls, you can change the Paper Textures. You can also check the Sample Merged box to apply these effects to every layer in the image. If it is not checked, only the active layer is affected.

4. If you only want the effect to apply to a specific part of the image, select it beforehand using a selection tool. You may also want to zoom in on the section.

5. Click, hold, and drag the primary mouse button to paint with the Retouch tool. If the effects are not fast or dark enough, increase the opacity.

6. When you have finished painting the line, release the mouse button. In **Figure 7.19** we used the Retouch tool to smudge out lines on a sunflower and emboss the veins in the leaves.

✔ Tip

■ To draw a straight line with the Retouch tool, click on the beginning point of the line, hold Shift and click where the ending point should be. A straight line is formed between these two points. Release Shift.

Figure 7.19 Hand applied filters are accomplished using the Retouch tool.

To set Paper Textures:

1. When you choose the Paintbrush, Color Replacer, Cloning, Retouch, Eraser, and Airbrush tools, the control panel appears (if not, press the letter O).

2. Click on the Tool Controls tab. Choose a Paper Texture from the drop-down box.

✔ Tip

■ See this book's Color Section for color examples of each Paper Texture type.

■ When you choose a texture, draw on the screen, and the texture appears, like a rubbing with your foreground color. **Figure 7.20** displays the available textures. For example, if the letter texture is chosen, and you have a blue foreground, the airbrush tool makes the image appear with the letters used as the line, with a little light blue mixed in to create a more solid line.

3. The more you paint over a texture, the more it shines through; but it eventually fills in solidly. Draw back over such areas with the right mouse button (background) or use the Eraser.

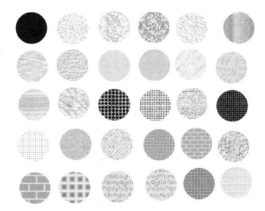

Figure 7.20 You can work on many varied paper textures.

Figure 7.21 The Fill Tool control panel.

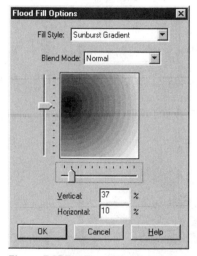

Figure 7.22 The Flood Fill Options dialog box lets you refine your fill options and preview the gradient.

Figure 7.23 A simple circular Gradient fill.

Filling and Gradients

The Fill tool lets you fill any specific area with a color, gradient, or pattern. An area may be defined by the selection tools or may be a continuous area of pixels sharing the same color, luminance, or other characteristic.

To use the Fill tool:

1. To begin filling an area, make a selection or, if you want to fill a specific color area, click on the Flood Fill tool. The control panel appears (if not, press the letter O).

2. Choose from several fill styles including a pattern, linear gradient, rectangular gradient and more (**Figure 7-21**).

3. Click on the Options button to experiment using the preview box (**Figure 7.22**). First select the match the mode that offers with RGB color, hue, brightness, or none. This determines the criteria under which pixels are replaced with the fill style you select.

   The Options box also lets you change the fill style and choose a blend mode. To the left of and under the preview box are the vertical and horizontal adjust bars.

4. Click on the control button and drag it until you get the desired look, or type in the desired percentages in the available boxes.

   Each fill style has its own adjustment controls. All the bars are easy to figure out—just play with them until you get the desired effect. When finished, click OK.

5. Once you select all your options, the Flood Fill tool adds a + symbol under the drip of the can, which means it is ready to fill the area with the desired effects. **Figure 7.23** shows a circular gradient.

6. Make sure the cursor is inside the target area, and click the primary mouse button.

To use an image to fill an area:

1. Open a new image on the screen.

2. Open an existing image, which will fill the selected area or background. Choose the Flood Fill tool and open its control panel.

3. In the Fill tool control panel, set fill style to Patterns and click the Options button.

   The responding dialog box lets you set pattern fill options. Important: choose the New Pattern Source. For the blend mode there are a number of options, such as normal, hue, lighten, darken, and more. The options are the same as those in the Layer dialog box. For more on blend modes, see Chapter 5.

4. Click on the drop-down menu and choose any image listed (in order to be selected, an image must be open).

   The picture box below presents a thumbnail of the image (**Figure 7.24**). Choose a blend mode and click OK. (For a plain fill of the actual picture, choose Normal.)

5. Shift back to your area in the image. Make sure the Fill tool is on and click inside the selection. The image appears in the area. If you are filling the entire background, and it is larger than the fill image, the image will tile in the background (see **Figure 7.25**)

✔ Tip

■ If you want to select a specific smaller area of an image as a pattern, copy the selection to a new image and then select that as your new pattern source. Follow all the same steps to fill the new area.

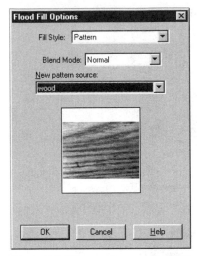

Figure 7.24 When you've set pattern fill options correctly, a thumbnail of the pattern appears in the flood fill preview dialog.

Figure 7.25 A simple house drawing using a wood texture that was filled in using pattern fill.

FILLING AND GRADIENTS

Figure 7.26 Select from two cloning modes: Aligned or Non-Aligned.

Cloning Areas

The Clone Brush is a great drawing tool. It can be used to replicate imagery from an area on a pixel-by-pixel basis. It can help you remove scratches from a photo by cloning over them or duplicate imagery and add it into a picture.

To use the Clone Brush tool:

1. Click on the Clone tool icon on the toolbar. The control panel should appear (if not, press the letter O). The Brush Tip options work the same as the Paintbrush tool's (see earlier in this chapter).

2. Once you select a brush style, choose a Clone mode as shown in **Figure 7.26**.

   The choices are Aligned or Non-Aligned. Aligned takes the source area from which you are deriving the image to be cloned and reproduces it exactly. When you draw, the originating point for the cloning source remains at a constant distance. If you move the mouse without drawing then press the primary button to begin drawing again, the brush clones each pixel that is the exact distance from the current point you're drawing on.

   For Non-Aligned, the image starts from the originally specified cloning source point every time the mouse is lifted and placed back down to draw again. This makes it easy to rapidly clone the same areas of an image in multiple areas of your image.

✔ Tip

- Check Sample Merged to clone all visible data, instead of just one layer. Unchecked, it only clones from the active layer. To use the Clone tool on a layer, make sure it is the active layer. You can also clone into a specific section. Select the section using one of the selection tools explained in

Chapter 4. In both cases, cloning only occurs in the specified area.

3. To set the cloning source point, place the cursor over the area you want to clone from. Hold down Shift while clicking on the area with the right mouse button. The computer beeps to let you know a clone area origin has been chosen. This selects the target area from which to copy.

4. Go to the area in the image on which you would like to paste the cloned image. It can can be the same image or a different one.

5. The area you just selected to have cloned (the source area) will have cross hairs on it once you begin copying the section to another location. This is to show you what area is being cloned as you move over the new area with the mouse.

6. Once you select a source point, begin cloning the imagery by drawing, using the primary mouse button. The cloning brush icon appears over the section on which the image is being placed down, and the cross hairs are over the source area. **Figure 7.27** shows a partially cloned Starfish created using the Clone tool.

7. When you finish copying the area, release the mouse button. Repeat as needed.

✔ Tips

■ In order to use the Clone tool, the image must be at least 24-bit color or grayscale.

■ The images you are using should be of equal color depth so the cloned area does not look out of place. The idea is to make a correction that is not noticeable.

Figure 7.27 The Clone tool in action.

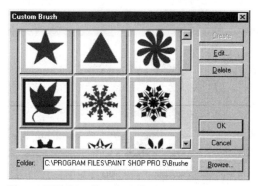

Figure 7.28 Paint Shop Pro offers unique custom brushes.

Custom Brushes

If you would rather paint with a star or cloud instead of a circle or square, choose one of the custom brushes.

To customize your brush tip:

1. Choose one of the brush tools on the tool palette that allows you to adjust the brush tips on the control panel.

2. Once the control panel is open, click on the Brush Tip tab. If the control panel does not open, press the letter O.

   In the Brush Tip section, click on the button that looks like a paintbrush tip. When the menu appears, select Custom. The Custom Brush dialog box appears (**Figure 7.28**). You have about 12 different options for brush tips, including a star, a leaf, a cloud, and so on. Select one.

3. Click OK. You can now begin drawing.

✔ Tips

- This custom brush shape will only work with the brush tool under which you chose it. For example, if you chose a custom brush using the Paintbrush tool, the same brush tip will not automatically work when you click on Airbrush. You must repeat the steps to choose a custom brush for each different painting or drawing tool.

- The tool draws or paints in the shape of the custom brush that was chosen. If you are using the Paintbrush tool and chose the star as your custom brush, the Paintbrush tool will paint in a star pattern. The stars will overlap and form a line as the cursor is dragged across the canvas (or click and release in one area for a single star shape).

Custom Brushes from Images

When the given custom brush selections do not suit your needs, take a section of an image and make it into a brush tip.

To create your own custom brush:

1. Open an existing image and select the area you want to make into a brush tip, using the selection tool. The selected area can be no larger than 255 x 255 pixels.

2. Click on any brush tool on the toolbar, which activates the Brush Tip section on the control panel. If the control panel does not open, press O on the keyboard.

3. Click on the Brush Tip tab on the control panel. In this section, click on the button that has the picture of a brush tip on it. When the menu appears, click on Custom. This opens the Custom Brush dialog box.

   The selected image should appear in a new box at the end, after all of the other boxes filled with custom brushes (**Figure 7.29**).

✔ Tip

■ When choosing or creating an image for a brush tip, make sure it is done in a dark enough color. If you use a color such as yellow, the image will be very faint; when you try to draw with this custom brush tip, it will draw faintly no matter what color you use. We suggest using black in the custom brush tip image. This will show off other colors you choose in their truest form when you draw with the custom brush.

Figure 7.29 You can turn any image or selection into a custom brush.

CUSTOM BRUSHES FROM IMAGES

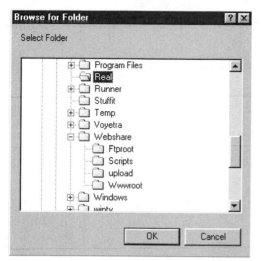

Figure 7.30 You must tell Paint Shop Pro which directory your custom brushes are in to be able to select them from the custom brush menu.

To save a custom brush:

1. To save the new brush tip to the default directory, click on the Create button in the Custom Brush dialog box. The default directory is Paint Shop Pro Brush folder. This is where all the Custom Brushes that come with Paint Shop Pro are stored.

When you click on the Create button, the image is stored in the Brush folder and is automatically placed on the list with the other Custom Brushes.

2. To save the image to a different folder, click on the Browse button in the dialog box. The Select Folder dialog box appears. Click on the name of the folder in which you want the Custom Brush to be stored and click OK.

The Select Folder dialog box disappears, and you return to the Custom Brush box.

✔ Tip

■ If you know the exact root or location where you want to store your Custom Brush, enter them into the Folder box at the bottom of the Custom Brush box.

To load custom brushes:

1. To use a previously saved custom brush, you must first load it. Select Custom... from the brush tip menu on the brush tool control box.

2. The Custom Brush dialog box appears and displays whatever custom brushes are stored in the current directory its tuned to.

Most of the time this will be the standard PSP custom brushes (the Brushes subdirectory of Paint Shop Pro). If the custom brushes do not appear when you arrive at the Custom Brush dialog box, click Browse and find the Brushes folder (**Figure 7.30**). Click OK, and the brushes appear.

If you would like to use one of the brushes you created yourself and saved in a different folder, browse to that folder and click OK.

3. Click on the image with which you would like to paint in the Custom Brushes dialog box. The selected image appears with a bluish-green outline. Click OK when you have selected the image you want. The Custom Brush dialog box disappears, and the image you chose loads and appears on the control panel in the viewing box.

✔ Tips

■ If you change painting tools, you must select a Custom Brush again.

■ To delete a Custom Brush, go to the Custom Brush dialog box and click Delete.

■ To edit a Custom Brush, in the Custom Brush dialog box click Edit. The Custom Brush Edit dialog box appears. You can use the slider to adjust the Step variable. Click OK when you are finished, and the Custom Brush Edit box closes and saves the Step value you determined.

Figure 7.31 You can turn any image or selection into a Picture Tube.

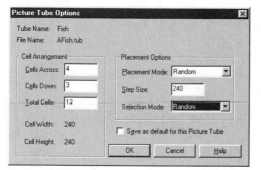

Figure 7.32 The Picture Tube Options dialog box lets you fine tune your picture tube settings.

Picture Tubes

Imagine that instead of painting with a simple brush, what poured out of your pen was a series of pictures, such as coins or pieces of popcorn. With Paint Shop Pro's Picture Tubes feature, you can do just that.

Paint Shop Pro contains a number of preset Picture Tubes, and new tubes can be added as well. Picture Tubes make it easy to paint with objects without having to create them each time you want to use them.

To use Picture Tubes:

1. Open a new or existing image.

2. Click on the Picture Tube tool on the Tools palette. The control panel opens as seen in **Figure 7.31** (if not, press the letter O).

3. Click on the Tool Controls tab. There are no adjustments for the Brush Tips.

4. Click on the Tube drop-down box to choose a Picture Tube. The standard choices are Coins, Letter Blocks, and Pointing Hands.

5. Drag the Scale slider to choose the percentage (10 – 250 percent) at which you want the Picture Tube objects to appear.

6. Click on the Options button at the bottom of the control panel. The Picture Tube Options dialog box opens (**Figure 7.32**). The Tube Name and the filename of the selected Picture Tube appear.

   The Cell Arrangement section allows you to change the placement of the Picture Tube objects on the page. In the Placement Options section, select Random or Continuous under the Placement Mode drop-down box. Random causes the program to spit out the objects with random placement; Continuous spaces the objects evenly along the page.

✔ Tip

■ Paint Shop Pro suggests using their default setting for the provided standard Picture Tube images.

7. By changing the Step Size, you can set the distance between Picture Tube objects. The distance between objects decreases when the Step Size decreases, and increases when the Step Size increases.

8. Change the Selection Mode by using its drop-down box. The choices are Random, Incremental, Angular, Pressure, and Velocity.

Random takes the images in the Tube and selects which one comes out at random. Incremental mode takes the first image in the tube and repeats after it selects all the images. Angular selects an image depending on which way the cursor is moved along the canvas. Pressure uses a pressure-sensitive pad and selects an image according to the amount of pressure applied. Velocity selects an image depending on how quickly or slowly you drag the cursor.

9. You can decide on settings for each particular Tube, and if you would like the same setting to appear every time you use that particular Picture Tube object, choose it as the default. To do this, check the Save As Default for this Picture Tube box.

10. When you have finished with all of the changes, click OK. The settings are available for use immediately.

11. Start drawing with the Picture Tube tool as you would with the Paintbrush tool. Click and drag the mouse in a particular direction. The images from the Picture Tube will appear on the canvas in the direction you are drawing (**Figure 7.33**).

Figure 7.33 Samples of picture tubes offered in Paint Shop Pro 5.

To create your own Picture Tubes:

1. Start by creating a grid of a size you desire. Go to the General Program Preferences (File>Preferences>General Program Preferences). The Paint Shop Pro Preferences dialog box appears.

2. Click on the Rulers and Units tab to bring it to the front. Make sure the Display Units are in pixels. The other option can stay on the default settings. (Default resolution is 72 pixels per inch.)

3. Determine how big you would like the boxes in the grid to be. Type the appropriate numbers in the Horizontal and Vertical spacing. The object cannot be any bigger than the cell size that you select. Remember these numbers for a later step.

4. The Line Color can be changed by clicking on the Change button. The Color dialog box appears. Choose any color from the color wheel. When you finish changing the color, click OK, and you return to the Paint Shop Pro Preferences dialog box.

5. When you finish all the grid specifications, click OK to close the dialog box.

6. Choose File>New or press Control-N. The New Image dialog box opens.

7. In the Image Dimension section, change the Width and Height to be multiples of the previously entered Horizontal and Vertical spacing from the Paint Shop Pro Preferences dialog box. This decides how many cells will be contained in the image.

   For example, if you choose 10 as your Horizontal and Vertical spacing numbers, then any number with a zero at the end would be a multiple. If you chose an image that was 100 in Width and Height, then you would have 100 cells total broken down into cells of 10 x 10 pixels.

Be sure the measurements are the same —if you use pixels as the grid form of measurement, they should all be in pixels.

8. Set the Background Color box to Transparent. After you make all the changes, click OK. The new image with the grid setup should appear (if not, choose **View>Grid**).

9. Gather or create the images you want in your picture cells as we did in **Figure 7.34**. Place one image per cell. These will be the images that come out one at a time from this Picture Tube. All the images placed in the cells of one document are considered a single Picture Tube.

10. When you have placed all the images in their cells, save your Picture Tube. Choose **File>Export>Picture Tube**. The Export Picture Tube dialog box appears (**Figure 7.35**).

11. In the Cell Arrangement section, enter the number of cells you created in the Cells Across and Down text boxes. Total Cells is figured automatically.

12. Select Placement mode in the Placement Options section. This can be changed later on when you use the Picture Tube, as explained in the previous section. In the Step Size box, enter the width of the cells in pixels. You can also change the Selection mode (see previous section).

13. Finally, type in the name you want for this Picture Tube in the Tube Name box.

14. When all the steps are completed, click OK. Paint Shop Pro adds the correct .tub extension to the file and places it in the Tubes Folder. It is also added to the Tube drop-down list in the Tool Controls in the Picture Tube control panel. You can now use it as we did in **Figure 7.36**

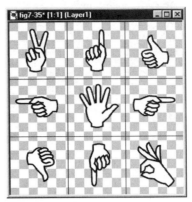

Figure 7.34 Our image is ready to be exported as a Custom Picture Tube.

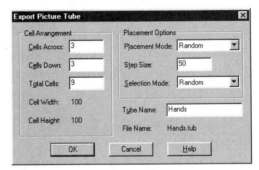

Figure 7.35 The Export Picture Tube dialog box.

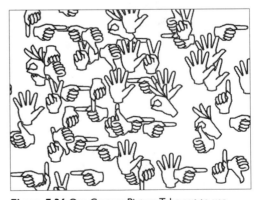

Figure 7.36 Our Custom Picture Tube put to use.

MASKS

The changes incorporated into Paint Shop Pro 5, such as support for layers and improvements in how selections work, have had a dramatic effect on the utility of masks. It may take a while to learn how to use masks to their full advantage, but once you do, you will appreciate the power and flexibility they offer.

In the version 4, masks were used to constrain operations to certain parts of the image. You can do that now with selections. As the option of creating layers was added to the program, the function of masks evolved.

In Paint Shop Pro 5.0, masks can be thought of as a stencil, like that used for a silk screen. Using masks, you can build a virtual stencil, and you decide what seeps through to lower layers and what doesn't.

Masks now open up possibilities for special effects that weren't available before.

Using Masks

Before you begin, let's review a key feature of selections. If you select a portion of any image using the selections tool, you can use filters or painting effects on an image or layer, and have them affect just that layer. In **Figure 8.1**, for example, we selected a square portion of an image and then painted around inside the selection. Any time we crossed outside the lines, the paint was prevented from "spilling" out. This feature of the selections tool is similar to the function masks served in the older versions of Paint Shop Pro.

Now masks are used to create effects on images like **Figure 8.2**. We painted over an image using a mask that let varying opacities of the paint "seep" through to the underlying image. This ability to vary opacity is what makes masks powerful.

In order to set this up, however, you need to understand how to create a mask. There are several ways to create a new mask. In every case, you want to have the mask reside on a separate layer within your image. Layers and masks go hand in hand, so if you feel you need to brush up on your layers skills, review Chapter 5.

To create a new mask:

1. Open an existing image or create a new one. Add a blank layer to that image and place the layer above the current image. For the purpose of learning about masks, we suggest a good photo as your image.

2. Make the new blank layer the active layer.

3. Go to the New section of the Masks menu (Masks>New). You will see several options—more if you've made an existing selection. For now choose Masks>New> From Image.

Figure 8.1 You can use selections to constrain painting or a filter effect to a specific area of the image.

Figure 8.2 Note how the car, repainted as it is, still maintains the luminosity of the original image because of the use of a mask.

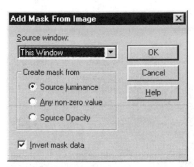

Figure 8.3 The Add Mask From Image dialog box.

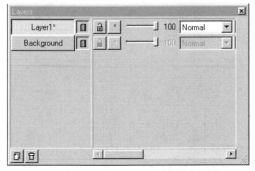

Figure 8.4 Layers with an asterisk (*) next to them have an active mask attached.

4. The Add Mask From Image dialog box appears (**Figure 8.3**). You can choose to create a mask from any currently open image using the listing in the Source Windows drop-down box. This makes it possible to edit a mask as a new image and then quickly use it in an existing image. Choose This Window to select the current image.

5. Next, you must choose which process to use to create the mask. With Source Luminance, the strength of masking is determined by how dark a pixel is. Darker pixels are masked more than lighter ones. The Any Non-zero Value option sets the mask to totally covered if a pixel is anything but perfectly white (R:0, G:0, B:0). Source Opacity sets the gradation of the mask depending on the opacity of the image.

6. If you want to invert the mask data, switching the intensity of areas, check the invert mask checkbox.

7. When you're done, press OK.

8. Your mask is now created and bound to the currently active layer. An asterisk (*) attached to the layer denotes that the layer has an active mask attached (**Figure 8.4**). You may have one mask per layer.

9. If your mask isn't visible (a red tint over the image) choose **Masks>View Mask** or Ctrl-Alt-V.

✔ Tip

■ To mask an entire layer solidly, choose **Masks>New>Hide All**. To unmask an entire layer, **Masks>New>Show All**.

To create a mask from a selection:

1. Load or create a new image and then create a new layer on that image.

2. Switch to the layer that contains the main area you want to select and make the selection using any one of the selection methods detailed in Chapter 4.

3. Once you've made a selection, switch the active layer to the new blank layer where you will create the mask.

4. Choose Masks>New>Hide All.

5. A solid mask should be created and displayed (**Figure 8.5**). If your mask isn't visible, choose Masks>View Mask or Ctrl-Alt-V.

✔ Tip

■ Masks work well with selections. Once you've activated your mask on one layer, you can create selections to limit the painting area. If you need to use the magic wand selection, switch layers to the underlying imagery to make your selection and then switch back to use your mask when painting over it.

Once you create a mask, you can save it to either a disk or Alpha Channel. Alpha Channel means the file can be used in other images. Once saved to a disk drive, the mask can be opened later in Paint Shop Pro as an image to be edited. Saving to an Alpha Channel saves the image within the image for later use.

To save a mask:

1. Select Masks>Save to Disk. This opens the Save Mask Channel dialog box.

   This box is similar to the Save or Save As dialog boxes common in Windows. The Save as Type is chosen for you, as PSP Mask Channel (*.msk). The information needed is the filename and the directory in which you want to save the file.

Figure 8.5 Before and after example using a selection to enable a mask.

An unmasked selected sky

After a mask is applied and displayed, a darker masked sky.

✔ Tip

- Try to keep your masks saved in the same folder for easy recovery.

2. Click Save. The mask is saved with the .msk extension in the specified folder.

To load a mask:

1. Open an image or create a new image. Select the layer to which you want the mask to be bound.

2. Choose **Masks>Load from Disk**. The Load Mask Channel dialog box opens.

3. This dialog box functions like the common File Open dialog box found in many Windows programs. Make sure the dialog box is pointing to the specific folder containing your .msk files.

4. When the correct folder is set, masks you've saved should appear in the list of files for this folder. Select the appropriate filename by clicking on it once.

5. The filename appears in the Filename box, and you can now click Open.

6. The image opens.

USING MASKS

Alpha Channels

An Alpha Channel saves masks and the information you want from selections. By saving
a mask or selection this way, you keep that
information within the image file.

To save to an Alpha Channel:

1. Create a mask. Then choose **Masks>Save to
   Alpha Channel**.

2. If you were editing your mask, you must
   turn off the Edit command in order to use
   the Save to Alpha Channel command.
   Once you select the command, the Save To
   Alpha dialog box appears (**Figure 8.6**).

3. Available Documents lists the documents
   from which you have made the mask. In
   the Available Alpha box, the blue highlighted name is the mask you just created.
   It should say New Channel.

4. The Preview box gives you a black and
   white preview of the masked area. The
   white area is masked, black is the open
   area. Click OK to continue.

5. The New Channel dialog box appears
   (**Figure 8.7**). This allows you to name the
   new mask that you just created. After filling out a name, click OK.

6. Both dialog boxes disappear, and the mask
   is saved as an Alpha Channel.

To load an Alpha Channel:

1. Open an image that has a mask saved
   within it as an Alpha Channel.

2. Select **Masks>Load from Alpha Channel**. The
   Load from Alpha dialog box appears
   (**Figure 8.8**).

3. From the Available Documents drop-down
   menu, select the name of the image from
   which you want to select the Alpha
   Channel. Your image must be open.

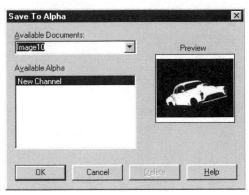

Figure 8.6 The Save To Alpha Channel dialog box.

Figure 8.7 Name your new channel using the New
Channel dialog box.

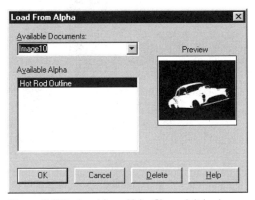

Figure 8.8 The Load from Alpha Channel dialog box.

ALPHA CHANNELS

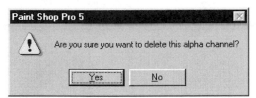

Figure 8.9 When deleting a mask you're given a last warning.

4. Once you select the image from the Available Documents list, the available Alpha Channels are listed.

5. When you click on the Alpha name, the mask appears in the Preview Box highlighted in blue.

6. Now that you have the appropriate Alpha Channel selected, click OK. The mask takes effect on the image.

To delete a mask from an Alpha Channel:

1. Open the image from which you want to delete the mask that is saved in an Alpha Channel.

2. Select **Masks>Load from Alpha Channel**. The Load from Alpha dialog box opens.

3. Select the image from the Available Documents drop-down menu.

4. Select the name of the mask you want to delete from the Available Alpha box.

5. Click on Delete. A warning box opens (**Figure 8.9**), asking you if you are sure you want to delete the selected mask. If you are certain, click Yes; if you want to check it out again, click No. The warning box closes, and you are returned to the Load from Alpha dialog box.

6. From the dialog box, you can open an existing mask or click Cancel to return to the image on which you were working.

Viewing and Editing Masks

Once you have created and saved a mask, you can perform any of a number of useful processes on it.

To view an active mask:

1. To see the mask you're working on, select Masks>View Mask or Control-Alt-V. A checkmark appears to the left of the command when the mask is being viewed.

2. The masked area appears with a reddish screen over the blank area where the masked image would be. **Figure 8.10** shows a plain image. **Figure 8.11** shows an image after a mask has been applied.

Inverting a mask just gives it the opposite effect. Areas of high masking become open, and vice versa.

To invert an active mask:

1. Create a mask.

2. Select Masks>Invert or press Shift-K.

3. The mask is immediately inverted (**Figure 8.12**).

To delete a mask from a layer:

1. When you have a mask loaded in an image and want to delete it, select Masks>Delete.

✔ Tip

■ If the mask is on a specific layer, you must select the layer before deleting.

2. A question box appears. The box asks if you would like to merge the mask into the current layer. Choosing Yes merges the mask, leaving a blank spot where the mask was. No removes the mask and places the contents that were under it back where they were. If an effect has affected the

Figure 8.10 A plain image with no mask.

Figure 8.11 An image with a mask actively displayed has a reddish tint over the masked area (okay, so it's dark gray in this figure).

Figure 8.12 Note from **Figure 8.11** that the previously masked area of the car is now brighter (unmasked) while the rest of the image is darker, showing off the inverted mask feature.

Figure 8.13 Using the edit mask feature we added more masked areas on the car which can be seen as newer darkened areas vs. that seen in Figure 8.11.

image, the effect now affects the masked area also. Cancel closes the box and allows you to resume working with the image.

To edit an active mask:

1. There are two ways to edit a mask. One is to change the area to be masked, and the other is to change the level of masking.

✔ Tip

■ Its always easier to edit the mask by viewing the mask first (Masks>View Mask or Control-Alt-V).

2. Select Masks>Edit or Ctrl-K.

3. Use the painting and drawing tools from the toolbar to alter the mask. Not all of them work with the mask function.

4. To change the masked area, select black for the foreground color and white for the background. To make the area masked, use the black; to erase the masked area, use the white. In **Figure 8.13** we took the original mask seen in **Figure 8.11** and masked in the tires, windows and front chrome using the paintbrush to edit the mask.

5. To create various levels of masking, paint with darker and lighter grays.

✔ Tip

■ Use the gradient fills for fun effects when editing a masked area.

6. Select Masks>Edit Mask or Ctrl-K. The checkmark next to the command disappears.

FILTERS

In this chapter we explore filters, one of the many ways to deform or improve imagery. Filters are used in graphics programs to change or enhance an image. Many different filters can be used within Paint Shop Pro. You can also use plug-in filters that come from third-party companies such as Kai's Power Tools (from MetaCreations) or Eye Candy (from Alien Skin Software). This chapter shows you how to use Paint Shop Pro's built-in filters as well as how to create your own custom filters.

What Filters Do

Filters change the appearance of an image by either changing the entire image or its borders. Filters can give an image a certain effect, such as blurring the image to help blend the colors together. Other filters can emboss an image to give it a 3-D look or make it appear to have a hot wax coating. You can combine two or more filters on a particular image to enhance it even more.

The only images to which filters can be applied are 24-bit color or grayscale images.

A filter works by analyzing each pixel and its surrounding area. Then, based on the criteria of the filter, it changes the color of the pixels to varying degrees, giving an entirely new look to the image. For example, an edge enhance filter looks for areas of extremely high contrast, such as a black line against a light gray background, and then enhances that line by making the pixels forming the line a little darker and the surrounding background a little lighter. A blurring filter examines each pixel and makes its color more closely match that of its neighboring pixels. Later on in this chapter, we explain how each type of filter works in more detail.

To apply a filter:

1. Choose an image or make a selection, as described in Chapter 4, to apply a filter to a specific portion of an image.

2. Under the Image menu you will find all the Filter choices. Determine which filter you want to run.

3. Once you have selected a filter it will either run immediately or it will present a dialog box (as shown in **Figure 9.1**) where specific characteristics of the filter can be further applied. (See **Figure 9.2** for a before and after example.)

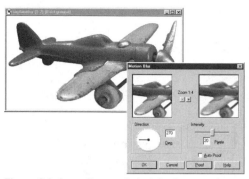

Figure 9.1 Some filters include dialog boxes with options you can select to further refine the filter's effects, like the Motion Blur filter shown in this example.

Figure 9.2 An example of an image before and after a filter has been run.

Before

After

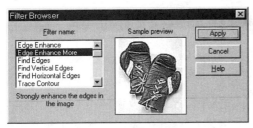

Figure 9.3 Paint Shop Pro's Filter Browser.

4. You can repeat the application of filters as often as you like to achieve the desired effects.

To use the Filter Browser:

1. The Filter Browser (as shown in **Figure 9.3**) gives you a quick and easy way to commonly apply any of the filters standard in Paint Shop Pro. Start by bringing up the Filter Browser dialog box (Image>Filter Image Browser).

2. Under Filter name, choose any of the standard filters for Paint Shop Pro.

3. Preview it before it is applied to the original image. The preview will be of the entire image, whether there is a selected area in the image or not.

4. To apply the chosen filter to the original image, click Apply.

5. To exit the dialog box without applying the filter, click Cancel.

THE FILTER BROWSER

As mentioned earlier, Paint Shop Pro comes with a number of standard filters. These are not the only filters that can be used with this program but tend to be the fairly standard processes you will use over and over. Understanding what each filter does, and how to use some of the more complex ones, is a critical part of learning all the ins and outs of Paint Shop Pro.

Blur Filters

Paint Shop Pro has six standard Blur filters: Blur, Blur More, Gaussian Blur, Motion Blur, Soften, and Soften More. Each essentially blends the pixels together for a smoother or blurrier image. Severely sharp imagery or high-contrast areas can be made to look a little more natural by blurring and blending sharper pixels together (see **Figure 9.4**).

To use the Blur filter:

1. Once you have the image or selected area, go to the Image menu, and choose Blur>Blur.

2. The filter will take effect on the image, lightly blurring the pixels together.

3. If the Blur is not enough, it can be repeated. For a coarser version, you can use the Blur More Filter.

To use the Blur More filter:

1. Once you have the image or selected area, go to the Image menu, and choose Blur More (Image>Blur>Blur More).

2. The filter runs an emphasized version of the traditional Blur filter.

Figure 9.4 The original image, processed with the Blur filter, and with the Blur More filter.

Original

Blur

Blur More

Figure 9.5 The original image and what it looks like after the Gaussian Blur filter has been applied.

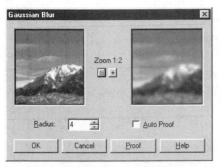

The Gaussian Blur filter

Original

Gaussian Blur

To use the Gaussian Blur filter:

1. Gaussian Blur gives you more control over how the blur process will affect the image. Start by choosing an image or making a selection and then starting the Gaussian Blur filter (Image>Blur> Gaussian Blur).

2. The Gaussian Blur dialog box appears (see **Figure 9.5**). This box has two preview boxes. The box on the left shows a sample area of the image before the filter has run, and the box on the right gives an example of what the image will look like after the Gaussian Blur has been applied.

3. In the Radius box the number can be increased or decreased. The higher the number, the greater the blur, and the lower the number, the less the blur will be. By checking the Auto Proof box, the Gaussian Blur will automatically appear on the image and in the right preview box on the Gaussian Blur dialog box. If auto proof is off, you can manually initiate a proof by clicking the Proof button on the dialog box.

4. Once you have the desired setting, click OK. If you click Cancel, the image will resume its original appearance without the Gaussian Blur effect.

BLUR FILTERS

To use the Motion Blur filter:

1. Motion Blur allows you to give the blur a specific directional emphasis, creating the appearance of movement. Start by choosing an image or making a selection and then starting the Motion Blur filter (Image>Blur>Motion Blur).

2. The Motion Blur Filter dialog box appears, as shown in **Figure 9.6**. It contains the two preview boxes, and lets you set the amount of blur. The Motion Blur filter also offers a feature not available on the Gaussian Blur filter: the Direction and Intensity options.

3. The Direction circle allows you to choose a direction in Degrees. Click on the marker line in the Direction circle. Hold the mouse and move in a circular direction until it has reached the appropriate direction and then release the mouse. Adding a new number to the Degree box can also change the degree setting.

4. The Intensity is measured in pixels. By either moving the Intensity slider bar or changing the value in the Pixels box you can increase or decrease the intensity of the motion effect. The higher the number, the greater the blur, and the further out the blur will go from the edge of the image or selection.

5. Once you have the desired setting, click OK. If you click Cancel, the image will resume its original appearance without the Motion Blur effect.

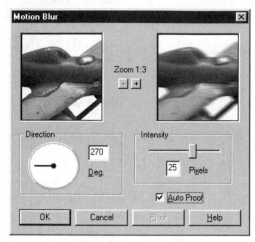

Figure 9.6 The Motion Blur filter in action.

Original

Motion Blur

BLUR FILTERS

Figure 9.7 The original image , passed through the Soften filter and as it looks passed through the Soften More filter.

Original

Soften

Soften More

The Soften filter does exactly what it says. It softens the image. If an image has sharp, rigid lines and you feel it stands out too much in relation to the rest of your work, you can soften the image so that the lines blend a bit better. There is no dialog box associated with this filter. Once it is chosen, it will take effect on the image.

To use the Soften filter:

1. Once you have the image or selected area, go to the Image menu and choose Blur> Soften.

2. After this filter is chosen, it will take effect on the image (see **Figure 9.7**).

3. You can repeat this filter if the imaged is not softened enough, or use the next filter, Soften More.

Soften More increases the softening of an image. This filter can be used in any order with other filters, and can be chosen first, if desired. It does not have to be used after the Soften Filter.

To use the Soften More filter:

1. Once you have the image or selected area, go to the Image menu, and choose Blur>Soften More.

2. After this filter is chosen, it will take effect on the image (see **Figure 9.7**).

3. You can repeat this filter if the image is not softened enough, or you can use it in any combination with other filters.

BLUR FILTERS

Edge Filters

Edge filters work to enhance the edges of an image. These filters affect the edges by emphasizing high-contrast areas of an image. Some Edge filters also distort the image into what looks like line art, extracting only the edges and not the "filler" of a picture.

Each filter in this category changes the image in its own way using the edges. Some use just the obvious edges that separate the foreground and background. Others use the edges of the pixels to distort the image.

To use the Edge Enhance filter:

1. The Edge Enhance filter makes the edges bolder and wider. It uses the contrast between dark and light to make the edges stand out. Once you have the image or selected area, go to the Image menu and choose Edge Enhance (Image>Edge> Enhance).

2. Once chosen, the filter takes effect on the image (see **Figure 9.8**).

3. You can repeat this filter if the edges are not enhanced enough, or use the Enhance More filter for a more obvious effect.

To use the Edge Enhance More filter:

1. If you're in need of stronger edge enhancement, use this filter. Once you have the image or selected area, choose the Enhance More filter from the menu (Image>Edge>Enhance More).

2. After this filter is chosen, it takes effect on the image (see **Figure 9.8**).

3. Repeat this filter as necessary.

Figure 9.8 The original image passed through the Edge Enhance filter and then passed through the Edge Enhance More filter.

Original

Edge Enhance

Edge Enhance More

Figure 9.9 The original image and the image passed through the Find filters.

Original

Find All

Find Horizontal

Find Vertical

To use the Find All filter:

1. The Find All filter finds all of the prominent edges in the image and makes only those lines visible.

2. After this filter is chosen, it will take effect on the image as shown in **Figure 9.9**.

3. If there are not enough edges shown, you can repeat the filter; alternately, you might run an edge enhance filter a few times first, and then run this filter.

To use the Find Horizontal filter:

1. This filter is similar to the Find All filter, except Find Horizontal concentrates only on horizontal edges in an image. Once you have the image or selected area, choose Find Horizontal from the menu (Image>Edge>Find Horizontal).

2. After this filter is chosen, it will take effect on the image.

3. If there are not enough edges shown, you can repeat the filter; alternately, you might run an edge enhance filter a few times first, and then run this filter.

To use the Find Vertical filter:

1. This filter is similar to the Find All filter, except it only finds vertical edges. Once you have the image or selected area, choose Find Vertical from the menu (Image>Edge>Find Vertical).

2. After this filter is chosen, it will take effect on the image.

3. If there are not enough edges shown, you can repeat the filter; alternately, you might run an edge enhance filter a few times first, and then run this filter.

To use the Trace Contour filter:

1. This edge filter attempts to create a line drawing representation of your image. Once you have the image or selected area, choose Trace Contour from the menu (Image>Edge>Trace Contour).

2. After this filter is chosen, it takes effect on the image as shown in **Figure 9.12**.

Figure 9.10 The original image and the image as it appears after being passed through the Trace Contour filter.

Original

Trace Contour

EDGE FILTERS

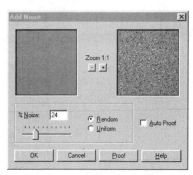

Figure 9.11 The Add Noise dialog box. The effect is shown in the next two images.

Original

Add Noise (Random)

Noise Filters

Noise filters deal with adding and subtracting high contrast spots to an image.

To use the Add Noise filter:

1. The Add Noise filter lets you add high contrast spots to an image. Once you have the image or selected area, choose Add Noise from the menu (Image>Noise>Add).

2. The Add Noise dialog box (**Figure 9.11**) appears. You can now choose the Noise percentage that dictates how much noise will be added to the image.

3. Choose whether the noise should be added randomly or in a uniform manner. Random noise produces color variance in the noise, and uniform noise produces single color noise.

4. When you have the desired settings, click OK.

NOISE FILTERS

To use the Despeckle filter:

1. Despeckle removes small points of high contrast from an image; it can be used to neatly clean up specks of dust from scans and other similar problems. Once you have the image or selected area, start the filter by choosing it from the menu (Image>Noise>Despeckle).

2. After this filter is chosen, it will take effect on the image (see **Figure 9.12**).

3. Repeat as needed to despeckle the image more.

✔ Tip

■ The Despeckle filter is quite useful to run after running other filters, as they can sometimes leave bits and pieces of high contrast noise on an image.

To use the Median Cut filter:

1. The Median Cut filter reduces bright and dark noise, and blends the image more by replacing lighter areas with darker colors. Start this filter by first choosing an image or selected area and then choosing Median Cut from the menu (Image>Noise>Median Cut).

2. After this filter is chosen, it will take effect on the image (see **Figure 9.13**).

Figure 9.12 Before and after shots, showing the Despeckle filter in action.

Original

Despeckle

Figure 9.13 Before and after shots, showing the Median Cut filter in action.

Original

Median Cut

Figure 9.14 The Sharpen filters in action.

Original

Sharpen

Sharpen More

Sharpen Filters

The Sharpen filters are used to create more variation between light and dark areas of the image, thus sharpening its overall appearance.

To use the Sharpen filter:

1. Once you have the image or selected area, choose Sharpen from the menu (Image>Sharpen>Sharpen).

2. After this filter is chosen, it will take effect on the image (see **Figure 9.14**).

3. Repeating this filter will increase the sharpening of the image. The Sharpen More filter can be used for a more pronounced effect.

To use the Sharpen More filter:

1. A stronger version of the basic Sharpen filter, you start this filter by choosing an image or selected area and then choosing Sharpen More from the menu (Image>Sharpen>Sharpen More).

2. After this filter is chosen, it will take effect on the image (see **Figure 9.14**).

3. Repeating this filter will increase the sharpening of the image.

SHARPEN FILTERS

To use the Unsharp Mask filter:

1. The Unsharp Mask filter lets you achieve a little more precision in your sharpening process. First select the image or area and then choose Unsharp Mask from the menu (Image>Shapen>Unsharp Mask).

2. The Unsharpen Mask dialog box appears (**Figure 9.15**). Choose the desired Radius, Strength, and Clipping factor. The greater the radius, the more pixels it will take into account when calculating the results. The strength determines the power of the process. Clipping helps reduce darker areas in the image—the higher the clip value, the more it reduces dark areas in the resulting image.

3. When finished, click OK.

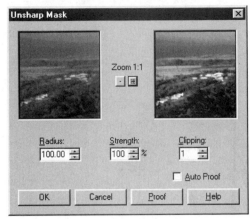

Figure 9.15 The Unsharp Mask filter in action.

Original

Unsharp Mask

Figure 9.16 Before and after shots showing the Dilate filter in action.

Original

Dilate

Figure 9.17 Before and after shots showing the Emboss filter in action.

Original

Emboss

Other Filters

These filters perform a variety of unique functions, allowing you to achieve special effects—they include the Dilate, Emboss, Erode, Hot Wax Coating, and Mosaic filters.

To use the Dilate filter:

1. Dilate increases the light areas of the image. Start this process by picking an image or a selected area and then choosing Dilate from the menu (Image>Other>Dilate).

2. After this filter is chosen, it takes effect on the image (see **Figure 9.16**). Light pixels expand into the darker area surrounding them.

3. Repeating this filter will increase the dilation of the image.

To use the Emboss filter:

1. Emboss takes a flat image, turns all the colors to medium gray and highlights its dominant images to give it a three-dimensional look. Once you have the image or selected area highlighted, choose Emboss from the menu (Image>Other>Emboss).

2. After this filter is chosen, it takes effect on the image (see **Figure 9.17**).

✔ Tips

■ Use the Negative color effect (Colors>Negative Image) to invert the look of your Emboss effect.

■ Run Trace Contours (Image>Edge>Trace Contour) first, then Erode (Image>Other>Erode), and then the Emboss filter for a distinctive effect.

The Erode filter makes the image look older. It adds dark areas in the sections between the dark and light.

To use the Erode filter:

1. The Erode filter expands dark areas of your image into lighter areas. Once you have the image or selected area highlighted, choose Erode from the menu (Image>Other>Erode).

2. After this filter is chosen, it takes effect on the image, adding pixels adjacent to the darker areas of the image (see **Figure 9.18**).

3. Repeatedly using this filter will increase the erosion effect; small lines can take several passes to achieve the effect you, might be seeking.

To use the Hot Wax Coating filter:

1. Hot Wax Coating makes an image look as if it had been rendered in a hot waxy substance. Begin by choosing an image or selected area to work with.

2. Make sure you have created a high-contrast difference between your foreground and background colors. Black foreground and white background tends to work well, but feel free to experiment with other colors.

3. Choose the Hot Wax Coating filter from the menu (Image>Other>Hot Wax Coating).

4. After this filter is chosen, it takes effect on the image (see **Figure 9.19**).

✔ Tip

■ Hot Wax Coating works best when the imagery and its surrounding area are high contrast, and when the colors in the image are more toward the bright side than not. It's also a great effect to use on type.

Figure 9.18 Before and after shots showing the Erode filter in action.

Orginal

Erode

Figure 9.19 Before and after shots showing the Hot Wax Coating filter in action.

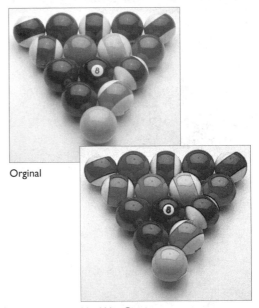

Orginal

Hot Wax Coating

Filters

Blur original

Blur

Gaussian Blur

Motion Blur

Blur 2 Original

Blur – Soften

Edge Original

Edge Enhance

Edge Enhance More

Edge Find All

Edge Find Horizontal

Edge Find Vertical

Edge Trace Contour

Noise Original

Noise Add

Noise Despeckle

Noise Median Cut

Sharpen Original

Sharpen

Unsharpen Mask

Other Original

Other Dilate

Other Emboss

Other Erode

Other Hot Wax Coating

Other Mosaic

Blends

Blend Dissolve

Blend Normal

Blend Darken

Blend Lighten

Blend Hue

Blend Saturation

Blend Color

Blend Luminance

Blend Multiply

Blend Screen

Blend Overlay

Blend Hard Light

Blend Soft Light

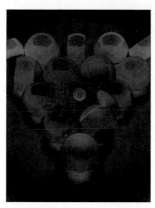

Blend Difference

Blend Dodge

Blend Burn

Blend Exclusion

Textures

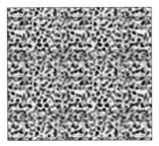

Paper Sidewalk

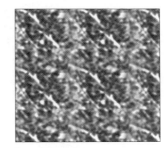

Paper Marble

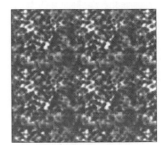

Paper Parchment

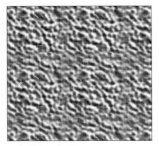

Paper Fruit Peel

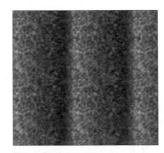

Paper Construction

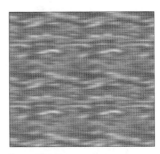

Paper Ocean

Paper Lava

Paper Mist

Paper Fog

Paper Cloud

Paper Marsh

Paper Wood grain

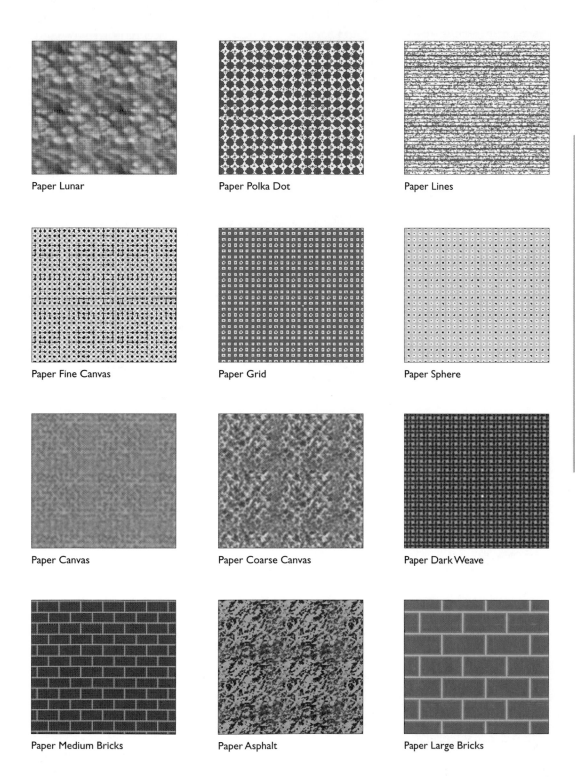

Paper Lunar

Paper Polka Dot

Paper Lines

Paper Fine Canvas

Paper Grid

Paper Sphere

Paper Canvas

Paper Coarse Canvas

Paper Dark Weave

Paper Medium Bricks

Paper Asphalt

Paper Large Bricks

Paper Daze

Paper Letters

Paper Letters 2

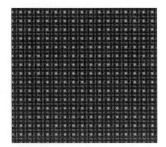

Paper Weave

Paper Small Bricks

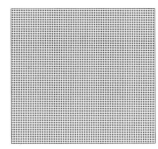

Paper Dither 25%

Paper Dither 50%

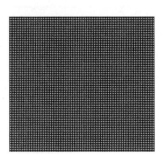

Paper Dither 75%

Figure 9.20 The Mosaic dialog box and before and after shots showing the Mosaic filter in action.

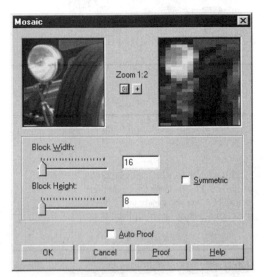

The Mosaic dialog box

Orginal

Mosaic

To use the Mosaic filter:

1. Once you have picked an image or a selected area of an image, choose Mosaic from the menu (Image>Other>Mosaic).

2. The Mosaic filter dialog box appears (**Figure 9.20**). Here you can design the size of the blocks that will make up the mosaic effect.

   Using the sliders, you can specify the Block Width and Height or you can change the number in the appropriate text boxes.

   By checking the Symmetric box, the Width and Height will be automatically set to the same number. Uncheck this box if you want to set different sizes for the Width and Height characteristics.

3. When you've got your desired settings, click OK to run the filter.

OTHER FILTERS

Defining Your Own Filters

Another great thing about Paint Shop Pro is that once you're tired of the built-in filters you can actually create your own.

Although creating your own filters isn't an easy process, an afternoon of experimentation with the User Defined Filters option in Paint Shop Pro can give you a world of new image processing possibilities.

To define your own filter:

1. Choose User Defined Filters from the menu (Image>User Defined Filters).

2. A Filter Browser dialog box appears (**Figure 9.21**) which presents you with a list of previously defined filters. You can click on any of those filters and then choose to Apply, Delete, or Edit them by pressing the appropriate buttons.

3. To create a new filter, click New.

4. The User Defined Filter Grid box appears (**Figure 9.22**). This is a 7x7 grid, into which you enter values. You will also see a box to assign a Division Factor designating a Bias Setting and a text box in which you enter your own name for the filter.

5. You can type integer values from −100 to 100 in these boxes. Patterns of numbers, as shown in **Figure 9.22**, tend to work best.

6. Set the division factor and the bias and press OK when you are finished.

7. Once you have entered a filter, you will return to the original User Defined Filters dialog box.

8. Select the filter that you want to run from the list of available filters.

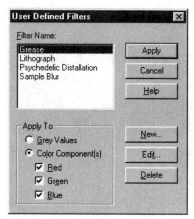

Figure 9.21 The User Defined Filter dialog box lets you create and administer your own custom filters for Paint Shop Pro.

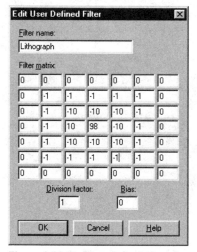

Figure 9.22 The User Defined Filter Grid is shown here with a filter design we got from Paint Shop Pro's Help file, which creates a lithographic design when run over an image. Concentric patterns like the one shown here tend to be the easiest to design.

Figure 9.23 Before and after shots showing our custom lithographic filter in action.

Orginal

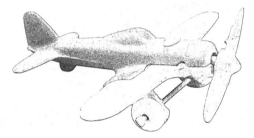

Custom lithograph

9. Decide if you want to apply the filter to the color channels in the image, or just to the gray values. When applying filters to the color channels, you may choose any or all of the red, green and blue channels.

10. Once you have your settings ready, press Apply to see it in action. We ran the previously mentioned lithographic filter over a toy airplane image as shown in **Figure 9.23**.

✔ Tips

■ The math behind User Defined Filters is too complex to explain it here. However, you are encouraged to check out Paint Shop Pro's Help file, which gives a great tutorial on the mathematical equation that drives the User Defined Filter process.

■ The best way to get the most out of User Defined Filters is to simply spend time experimenting with different filter patterns. When you find some that work, experiment by creating derivative versions of them. Over time, you will steadily build up some usable filters.

■ Remember also that filters that seem not to work on some images may work better on others. For example, a filter that tends to brighten everything will merely turn a bright image almost completely white—yet it might work well with very dark images. We suggest testing your filters on a bright test image, something fairly middle of the road, and something on the dark side.

Importing Filters into Paint Shop Pro

Paint Shop Pro can run any Photoshop-compatible plug-in. In addition to the plug-ins that come from third parties such as Kai's Power Tools from Metacreations, you can find hundreds of free or shareware-based filters available on the Internet.

The trick in using third-party and freeware/shareware filters is twofold. First, you must obtain the filters and make sure they are in the .8bf format that makes them Photoshop-compatible. Then you must tell Paint Shop Pro where these filters are located. As discussed in Chapter 2, you can configure up to three separate folders where Paint Shop Pro looks for extra filters. Once installed properly, the filters appear on your Image menu.

To convert filters to .8bf format:

1. First you need to find filters on the Internet. The majority of these filters are stored in a special format known as .FFL. Filters are stored in .FFL format so they can be converted into several popular filter formats. We suggest the following filter sites:

   http://pico.i-us.com/

   http://pluginhead.i-us.com/

   http://privat.schlund.de/filter-factory/

   These sites are good places to find filters, especially the popular Filter Factory Filters, and those created by Andrew Buckle. Among these three sites you'll find nearly 3,000 filters you can install for use with Paint Shop Pro.

2. The filters are usually zipped, so if you plan to download and use them you'll need to have an unzipping program such as WinZip (**www.winzip.com**), as seen in **Figure 9.24**, to unarchive them and save them to a directory.

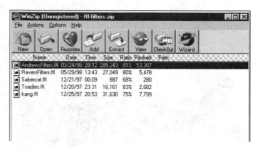

Figure 9.24 Unzip your filters.

Figure 9.25 The Plug-in Commander Web site.

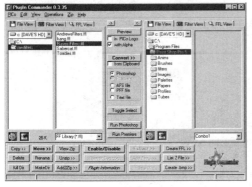

Figure 9.26 Plug-in Commander in action.

3. Once you've downloaded the .FFL files and saved them to a directory, you're ready to convert them to .8bf format.

4. To convert .FFL files to .8bf filters that are compatible with Paint Shop Pro, you'll need a copy of the premier filter conversion program— Harald Heim's awesome Plug-in Commander. You can download Plug-in Commander from his Web site (see **Figure 9.25**) located at: http://pico.i-us.com/. Download and install this program.

5. Once you've downloaded and installed Plug-in Commander, as well as a number of .FFL files, you're ready to convert them.

6. Launching Plug-in Commander, you'll find a medium-size window filled with two major windows split into two vertical lists and a ton of buttons (**Figure 9.26**). Plug-in Commander can do quite a few things, but we're just going to concentrate on a few key items to accomplish the task of converting the .FFL files into usable filters.

Plug-in Commander works with two major windows known as Tab Sheets; above each one there are tabs you can click on to see different views of the files you're working on.

The left side of the program is where you can open .FFL files and select the specific filters you wish to convert, while the right side shows the files you have converted. Each of these major windows can be set to one of three views: a File View, a Filter View and a .FFL file view.

7. Start by loading in a .FFL file to begin conversion. Do this by bringing the left window's File View tab to the forefront and setting the directory it points at to the directory where you extracted your .FFL files. When you do this correctly you will be greeted by a list of .FFL files in the adjacent list box. Choose any of the .FFL files by double-clicking on any file.

8. Plug-in Commander will automatically bring up a list of filters contained in that .FFL file. Here you may select any or all of the specific filters you want to export to .8bf format.

9. Once you've selected the files you want to import, you will notice in the middle of the screen that the Convert button is now bolded. Clicking on the Convert button will convert the selected filters to Photoshop format. Make sure the list just below the Convert button is set to Photoshop.

10. Once you are satisfied with your selections, click on the Convert button. Repeat this process until you've converted everything you want. Then exit Plug-in Commander.

11. If you're currently running Paint Shop Pro, exit and rerun the program so it will recognize the filters. Remember that, as shown in the Preferences section of Chapter 2, you need to tell Paint Shop Pro specifically into which directories you've placed the filters.

12. When you've installed filters correctly you will notice that on the Image menu below the User Defined Plug-in choice is a new one titled Plug-in Filters (see **Figure 9.27**), which will lead you to a list of all other third-party filters available to you.

✔ Tip

- Plug-in Commander is a great program that does more than just merely convert filters. You can edit them and do much more. We can't cover every last aspect of the program here. You're encouraged to read the Help files and tutorials located on the Plug-in Commander Web site located at: http://pico.us-i.com.

Figure 9.27 When you've installed filters correctly, they appear on the Image menu.

EFFECTS
AND DEFORMATIONS

Whereas *filters* change an image by altering the colors of each pixel, *deformations* and *effects* let you physically change the shape of the image or add useful elements to it.

Deformations let you shape images into different geometric forms, such as circles, cylinders, and pentagons.

Effects let you add special highlights to an image, such as chiseled outlines, drop shadows, or cutout highlights.

Arithmetic, a higher-end feature, lets you creatively merge together two pictures in ways not possible through layers and other cut and paste means.

Together, these provide Paint Shop Pro with some truly unique features not found in even some of the fancier graphics packages.

Deformations

Deformation effects focus mostly on common geometric shapes. At first glance only a couple of them seem useful, but try combining them to achieve interesting effects.

To apply a Circle deformation:

1. Choose the image or selection to which you want to apply a Circle deformation.

2. Choose Image>Deformation>Circle (**Figure 10.1**).

To apply a Cylinder deformation:

1. Choose the image or selection to which you want to apply a Cylinder deformation.

2. Pick and run either the Cylinder-Vertical (Image>Deformation>Cylinder-Vertical) or Cylinder-Horizontal (Image>Deformation>Cylinder-Horizontal) deformation process.

3. The Cylinder deformation dialog box appears (**Figure 10.2**), allowing you to set how prominent the effect will be. A slider below the preview box controls lets you set the percentage of the effect.

4. If you'd like to preview the deformation on the image itself, click the Auto Proof checkbox.

5. When you are satisfied with the setting, press OK to apply the deformation. **Figures 10.3** and **10.4** show the effects of the deformations on a hot dog image.

Figure 10.1 The original image, and the image after being passed through the Circle deformation.

Before

After

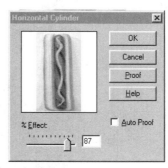

Figure 10.2 Both the horizontal (shown here) and vertical deformation dialog boxes are exactly alike.

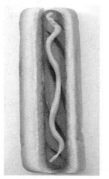

Figure 10.3 The horizontal deformation in action.

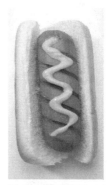

Figure 10.4 The vertical deformation in action.

Figure 10.5
The Pentagon deformation applied to the pool ball image.

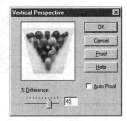

Figures 10.6 The Horizontal and Vertical Perspective dialog boxes.

Figure 10.7 The Horizontal and Vertical Perspective deformations applied to an image.

Horizontal Perspective deformation

Vertical Perspective deformation

To apply a Pentagon deformation:

1. Choose the image or selection to which you want to apply a Pentagon deformation.

2. Choose Image>Deformation>Pentagon (**Figure 10.5**).

To apply a Perspective deformation:

1. Choose the image or selection to which you want to apply a Perspective deformation.

2. Pick and run either the Perspective-Horizontal (Image>Deformation>Perspective –Horizontal) or Perspective-Vertical (Image>Deformation>Perspective-Vertical) deformation process.

3. The Perspective deformation dialog box appears (**Figure 10.6**), allowing you to set how prominent the effect will be. A slider below the preview box controls lets you set the percentage of the effect.

4. If you'd like to preview the deformation on the image itself, click the Auto Proof checkbox.

5. When you are satisfied with the setting, click OK to apply the deformation (**Figure 10.7**).

DEFORMATIONS

To apply a Pinch deformation:

1. Choose the image or selection to which you want to apply a Pinch deformation.

2. Choose Image>Deformation>Pinch.

3. The Pinch deformation dialog box appears (**Figure 10.8**), allowing you to set how prominent the effect will be. A slider below the preview box controls lets you set the percentage of the effect.

4. If you'd like to preview the deformation on the image itself, click the Auto Proof checkbox.

5. When you are satisfied with the setting, click OK to apply the deformation (see **Figure 10.9**).

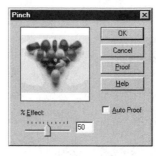

Figure 10.8 The Pinch deformation dialog box.

Figure 10.9 Pinch deformation applied to an image.

To apply a Punch deformation:

1. Choose the image or selection to which you want to apply a Punch deformation.

2. Choose Image>Deformation>Punch.

3. The Punch deformation dialog box appears (**Figure 10.10**), allowing you to set how prominent the effect will be. A slider below the preview box controls lets you set the percentage of the effect.

4. If you'd like to preview the deformation on the image itself, click the Auto Proof checkbox.

5. When you are satisfied with the setting, click OK to apply the deformation (**Figure 10.11**).

Figure 10.10 The Punch deformation dialog box.

Figure 10.11 Punch deformation applied to an image.

To apply a Skew deformation:

1. Choose the image or selection to which you want to apply a Skew deformation.

2. Choose Image>Deformation>Skew.

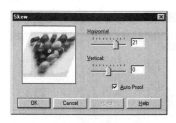

Figure 10.12
The Skew deformation dialog box.

Figure 10.13
Skew deformation applied to an image.

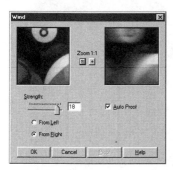

Figure 10.14
The Wind deformation dialog box.

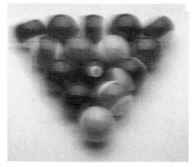

Figure 10.15 Wind deformation applied to an image.

3. The Skew deformation dialog box appears (**Figure 10.12**), allowing you to set the type and angle of the Skew deformation. Two sliders positioned in the box let you set either a horizontal skew or a vertical skew with an angle of –45 to +45 degrees. You cannot set both; thus, as soon as you move one of the two sliders, the other slider automatically resets to 0.

4. If you'd like to preview the deformation on the image itself, click the Auto Proof checkbox.

5. When you are satisfied with the settings, click OK to apply the deformation (**Figure 10.13**).

To apply a Wind deformation:

1. Choose the image or selection to which you want to apply a Wind deformation.

2. Choose Image>Deformation>Wind.

3. The Wind deformation dialog box appears (**Figure 10.14**), allowing you to set the type and angle of the Skew deformation. A slider in the box marked Strength lets you set the power setting for the Wind deformation from 1 to 20. You can also choose the direction from which the wind is blowing (left or right).

4. If you'd like to preview the deformation on the image itself, click the Proof checkbox.

5. When you are satisfied with the settings, click OK to apply the deformation (**Figure 10.15**).

✔ Tip

■ Seems the folks at Jasc never thought people might want to have the Wind blowing in at different angles (or even up or down for that matter). By rotating the image, applying the filter, and then rotating it back, you can achieve these alternative effects.

DEFORMATIONS

To use the Deformation Browser:

1. Select an image or a portion of an image to deform.

2. Choose **Image>Deformation>Deformation Browser**. The Deformation Browser appears (**Figure 10.16**).

3. In the Deformation name list, choose the deformation effect you'd like to apply. Note that you won't be able to tweak any of the deformations when you use the browser. If you'd like to play with the settings offered by some of the deformation varieties, run them individually.

4. Each effect, when selected, is previewed in the sample preview box next to the list.

5. Once you find the effect you'd like to apply, click on the Apply button, and the deformation is applied to the image.

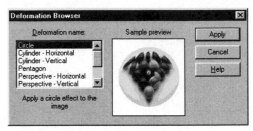

Figure 10.16 The Deformation Browser.

Arithmetic

Image arithmetic lets you combine pixels from two separate images, creating a third image that is the product of the combination. First, the images are made the same size (the second image is resized to the size of the first image if they do not share the same proportions). Then the program goes pixel-by-pixel through each image, performing a math function using the values of the corresponding pixels on each image. The resulting value is then used to determine the color of the pixels on the new image.

To understand this, let's look at the math involved and how two differently colored pixels produce a new colored pixel. We can perform nine specific mathematical functions on these two pixels to create the new color of the new pixel. These functions (and the math they create) include:

Add: New Pixel Value = Pixel A Value + Pixel B Value

Subtract: New Pixel Value = Pixel A Value − Pixel B Value

Multiply: New Pixel Value = Pixel A Value x Pixel B Value

Difference: New Pixel Value = Absolute Value of (Pixel A Value − Pixel B Value)

Lightest: New Pixel Value = Maximum of (Pixel A Value, Pixel B Value)

Darkest: New Pixel Value = Minimum of (Pixel A Value, Pixel B Value)

Average: New Pixel Value = (Pixel A Value + Pixel B Value)/2

Or: New Pixel Value = Binary Or

And: New Pixel Value = Binary And

ARITHMETIC

Let's plug in some values to see what's going on mathematically. Consider two pixels, A and B, and the RGB values for each.

A   **B**
R: 123   R: 34
G: 56   G: 98
B: 212   B: 176

Now look at the functions listed and do the math to see what the new pixel value will be if we choose the Add function:

A B   **Operation**   **New Pixel Value**

Add: R: 123 + R: 34   R: 157
       G: 56 + G: 98   G: 154
       B: 212 + B: 176   B: 378

Notice that the resulting pixel has a blue value of 378. However, the maximum value it can have is 255. That's where Clip Color Values comes into play. The Clip Color Values setting determines how Paint Shop Pro resolves color values greater than 255 or less than 0.

There are two settings for Clip Color Values: on or off. If the setting is on, it sets all values greater than 255 to 255, and all values lower than 0 to 0. If the value is off, it sets all values greater than 255 to be the original value minus 256; for all values less than 0, the resulting value is the original value plus 256. For the blue value (378) of the new pixel in the earlier example, here's a quick illustration of what the two settings will produce:

On: 378 is greater than 255, new value = 255

Off: 378–256, new value = 122

Now that you understand what's going on, take a look at **Table 10.1**, which shows how all the math works out for each function available in Paint Shop Pro.

Table 10.1

Function		Pixel A Value		Pixel B Value	New Pixel Value	Clip Color Value Setting On	Off
Add		R: 123	+	R: 34	= R: 157	R: 157	R: 157
		R: 56	+	R: 98	= R: 154	R: 154	R: 154
		R: 212	+	R: 176	= R: 378	R: 255	R: 122
Subtract		R: 123	+	R: 34	= R: 89	R: 89	R: 89
		R: 56	+	R: 98	= R: -42	R: 0	R: 214
		R: 212	+	R: 176	= R: 36	R: 36	R: 36
Multiply		R: 123	+	R: 34	= R: 4182	R: 255	R: 86
		R: 56	+	R: 98	= R: 5488	R: 255	R: 112
		R: 212	+	R: 176	= R: 37312	R: 255	R: 192
Difference	Abs. value:	R: 123	+	R: 34	= R: 89	R: 89	R: 89
	Abs. value:	R: 56	+	R: 98	= R: 42	R: 42	R: 42
	Abs. value:	R: 212	+	R: 176	= R: 36	R: 36	R: 36
Lightest	Maximum of:	R: 123	+	R: 34	= R: 123	R: 123	R: 123
	Maximum of:	R: 56	+	R: 98	= R: 98	R: 98	R: 98
	Maximum of:	R: 212	+	R: 176	= R: 212	R: 212	R: 212
Darkest	Minimum of:	R: 123	+	R: 34	= R: 34	R: 34	R: 34
	Minimum of:	R: 56	+	R: 98	= R: 56	R: 56	R: 56
	Minimum of:	R: 212	+	R: 176	= R: 176	R: 176	R: 176
Average		R: 123	+	R: 34	= R: 78	R: 78	R: 78
		R: 56	+	R: 98	= R: 77	R: 77	R: 77
		R: 212	+	R: 176	= R: 194	R: 194	R: 194
Or		R: 123	+	R: 34	= R: 123	R: 123	R: 123
		R: 56	+	R: 98	= R: 122	R: 122	R: 122
		R: 212	+	R: 176	= R: 244	R: 244	R: 244
And		R: 123	+	R: 34	= R: 157	R: 34	R: 34
		R: 56	+	R: 98	= R: 154	R: 32	R: 32
		R: 212	+	R: 176	= R: 378	R: 144	R: 144

ARITHMETIC

To use Arithmetic:

1. Create or load two images you want to combine together via Arithmetic.

2. Choose **Image>Arithmetic**. The Arithmetic dialog box appears (**Figure 10.17**).

3. Choose the first source image and the second source image from the drop-down lists at the top of the dialog box. Remember that if you do a subtraction function, order does matter.

   Order also matters if the two images you are combining are not the same size. If not, Paint Shop Pro automatically resizes image 2 to match image 1. (Note that just below the source image drop-down lists is text that displays the size of the resulting new image when the operation is complete.)

✔ Tip

■ We recommend resizing your imagery before combining. This way you get the best control and positioning. Letting Paint Shop Pro arbitrarily resize things for you doesn't always give you the best results.

4. Choose the function to run.

5. Determine the channels on which you are going to run the functions. All Channels is the default setting, but if you uncheck it you can individually select to combine any one channel of each image into the resulting image.

6. Set the modifiers.

   Divisors divide the resulting value by its setting. This takes effect before the out-of-range values are reset as directed by the Clip Controls setting. In general, higher settings should reduce the overall effect of the arithmetic transformations.

   The Bias modifier simply adds that value to the resulting value, but takes effect after the out-of-range values are reset as directed

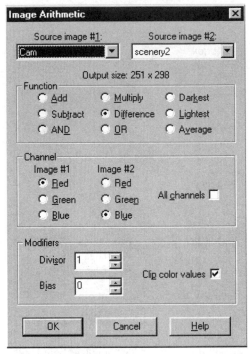

Figure 10.17 The Arithmetic dialog box.

Figure 10.18 Setup: Note the gray background around Dave and Cameron, which affects the lightness of the resulting image (white would wash out the entire background of the resulting image).

Figure 10.19 The resulting image combines the background with the image of Dave and Cameron.

by the Clip Controls setting. By setting the Bias to a positive value of 1 or more you will lighten the resulting image; −1 will darken the resulting image.

7. Set the Clip Color Values setting. If it's unchecked, it is off; checking the box turns it on. See earlier in this chapter for how this affects the resulting color values of the new image.

8. When satisfied with the results, click OK.

9. Paint Shop Pro calculates the results, first resizing the second source image if necessary and then doing the image arithmetic, and finally outputting the resulting picture as a new unnamed image. Press Esc at any time during calculation to abort the process. **Figures 10.18** and **10.19** demonstrate the setup and results of using the Add arithmetic function to combine two photos together.

Effects

Paint Shop Pro 5.0 offers users four major effects processes:

Buttonize: Makes it easy to develop 3-D styled graphics for use as graphical buttons on a Web page.

Chisel: Lets you add a chiseled look to imagery.

Cutout: Cuts the selected area out of the image.

Drop Shadow: Makes it easy to add a fine drop shadow effect.

Together, the four effects give you some flexible options for developing imagery. These are all particularly handy for creating imagery for your Web site — something covered in detail in Chapters 13 and 14.

To use the Buttonize effect:

1. Begin by making a selection using any of the selection tools from the menu (for more on selections, see Chapter 4).

2. Once you have made a selection, choose Buttonize from the Image menu (**Image> Effects>Buttonize**). The Buttonize dialog box appears (see **Figure 10.20**).

3. The Buttonize dialog box contains three main sliders and several options that let you set the characteristics of the effect. A Preview box and Auto Proof checkbox give you the ability to preview the effect on the selection.

4. Choose the shape of the button edges. The sliders for Height and Width control the thickness of the button's beveled edges on either the top and bottom (height) or the left and right sides (width). You can set the edge thickness up to the height or width of the selection, but the optimal settings are 2–5 percent of the image's width or height.

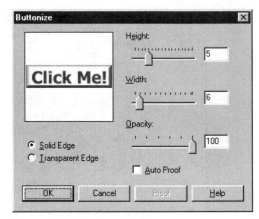

Figure 10.20 The Buttonize dialog box.

Figure 10.21 The image resulting from the Buttonize process.

5. After you've selected the height and width of the button sides, you need to define how those sides look. Just below the preview box are two options: Solid Edge or Transparent Edge.

Transparent doesn't disturb the underlying color of that area of the selection but merely creates a dark-to-light gradient for the beveled effect. Solid creates a solid edge also slightly gradated from dark to light except it ignores the underlying colors and creates a beveled edge substituting the current background color instead.

✔ Tip

■ If you use the solid edge option, be sure to select the desired edge color by changing the background color to the desired hue *before* initiating the Buttonize command.

6. After choosing a solid or transparent edge, you can affect the strength of that edge by changing its opacity. To create a lighter-looking edge, slide opacity lower by moving it to the left. For a darker edge, move opacity toward 100 by moving the slider toward the right. When you are satisfied with the results, click OK to complete the process. **Figure 10.21** shows the results of the Buttonize process.

✔ Tip

■ The Buttonize command only creates rectangular-shaped buttons and does not create the desired effects on irregularly shaped selections.

Chisel attempts to create the appearance that the edge of a selection has been chiseled out of stone or some other substance.

EFFECTS

To use the Chisel effect:

1. Make a selection using any of the available selection methods.

2. Choose Image>Effects>Chisel. The Chisel dialog box appears (**Figure 10.22**).

3. The Chisel dialog box contains a preview of the effect, a slider to determine the width of the effect, and the option to use a transparent or solid edge.

4. Set the width of the Chisel effect by sliding the slider up or down the scale. You may also enter a direct value into the provided text box located above the slider.

   Note that chisels for large selections of ten or more may take some time to preview and apply. Be careful with the size of the chisel, or prepare to wait.

5. Decide whether you want a solid edge using the background color or a transparent edge that darkens the pixels to create the chisel effect but does not change their hue. Once you are satisfied with the results, click OK or press Enter.

✔ Tips

■ The Chisel effect is one you need to experiment with to appreciate. It takes a lot of fine-tuning to get a good result. One aspect that discourages people from using it is how it looks around a photographic image (**Figure 10.23**). But if you change the selection to a solid image or some other non-photorealistic interior, the overall appearance of the resulting image is interesting.

■ We created **Figure 10.24** by selecting the outline of the image and applying a Chisel of about 16 pixels. Then we deleted the interior and applied Hotwax and Sharpening filters. Using a brown hue, we achieved a woodcut-style image that shows off the 3-D effect of the Chisel.

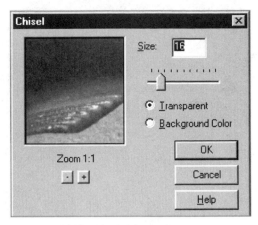

Figure 10.22 The Chisel dialog box.

Figure 10.23 Chisel is not very useful with photorealistic imagery.

Figure 10.24 Using Chisel in conjunction with other tools shows its true usefulness rather than what you see in Figure 10.23.

EFFECTS

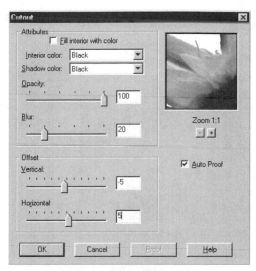

Figure 10.25 The Cutout dialog box.

Figure 10.26 The Cutout effect helps create some dark highlights.

✔ Tips

■ The Cutout effect is an excellent way to add highlights to images. It's also useful for creating interesting text effects, as shown in Chapter 11.

■ For a nice highlight edge, use light or dark settings with Cutout. We created the black edge highlights on the sunflower shown in **Figure 10.26** using a black-colored shadow, opacity of 100, blur of 20, vertical offset of −10, and horizontal offset of 5.

To use the Cutout effect:

1. Create a selection using any of the available selection tools.

2. Choose **Image>Effects>Cutout**. The Cutout dialog box appears (**Figure 10.25**).

   There are quite a few options and values you can set when using the Cutout effect. These include setting the color, blur and opacity of shadow and interior, and the amount the interior image is offset to create the Cutout effect.

3. Choose whether or not the interior of the selection is filled or left as the image. If you want to set a fill color, check the Fill Interior with Color checkbox.

4. To set interior color, choose from the drop-down selection among foreground, background, white, black, red, green, and blue.

5. Choose the shadow color among foreground, background, white, black, red, green, and blue.

6. Once you choose the interior and shadow colors, you may choose the opacity and the blur of the shadow. Slide the opacity down (to the left) to create transparency between the shadow and the interior image. Slide the blur up to create a finer gradient transition for the shadow effect. Note that high blurs of 15 or more can take some time to compute.

7. Choose the offset values that determine the look of the cutout. Each slider or associated text box can be set from −100 to 100. The offset will shift the cutout and shadow as defined by you.

8. Once you have the desired effect, click OK or press Enter to apply it.

EFFECTS

To use the Drop Shadow effect:

1. Create a selection using any of the available selection tools. Note that the drop shadow is created outside of the selection area and does not disturb it.

2. Choose Image>Effects>Drop Shadow. The Drop Shadow dialog box appears (**Figure 10.27**).

3. Choose the color of the drop shadow among foreground, background, white, black, red, green, and blue.

4. Once you've chosen the shadow color, you may choose the opacity and the blur of the shadow. Slide the opacity down (to the left) to create transparency between the shadow and underlying pixels. Slide the blur up to create a finer gradient transition for the shadow effect. Note that high blurs of 15 or more can take some time to compute.

5. Set the offset values that determine the positioning of the shadow. Each slider or associated text box can be set from −100 to 100. The offset will shift the shadow. To shift it to the left and below the selection, use negative values; to shift it to the right and above the image, use positive values.

6. Click OK or press Enter to apply it. **Figure 10.28** shows the Drop Shadow effect.

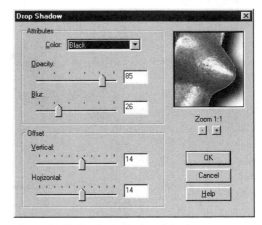

Figure 10.27 The Drop Shadow dialog box.

Figure 10.28 The Drop Shadow effect in action.

TYPE

You might want to create some eye-catching type effects for your Web page, or for a presentation. Perhaps you'd like to create your own logo, design a graphical heading, or add some visual interest to a title to spice up a Powerpoint slideshow.

Paint Shop Pro 5 lets you do quite a bit with type styles. In this chapter we'll cover the basics of the Type tool, and show you how to achieve some extra special effects using type.

Placing Down Type

Placing down type involves activating the Type tool and working through the responding dialog box, which allows you to set the various type attributes.

However, before beginning this process make sure you set the foreground color you want for the type, because you can't set it in the Type dialog box. The current foreground color will be the color of the type.

To place down type:

1. Select the image or start a new image.

2. Select the Type option on the left side tool bar or column. A (+A) symbol will appear when you move the cursor over the image area.

3. Click in the general area where you want the type to appear. The Add Text dialog box comes up (see **Figure 11.1**).

4. Type in the words you want to use. A sample of the text, in the chosen font style, will appear in the middle of the Add Text box. (It will say "sample of selected font at 1:1 zoom" above the box area.)

5. Under Font attributes are four boxes:

   Name: The actual type style can be chosen from this list.

   Style: This list controls the font's appearance (i.e., regular, *italic*, **bold**, **bold italic**, etc.)

   Script: This drop-down list lets you select the language script for the font— a useful feature if you want to switch to different language versions of a particular font.

   Size: You can set how large or small you would like your text to be. Note that while the list only goes up to 72 points,

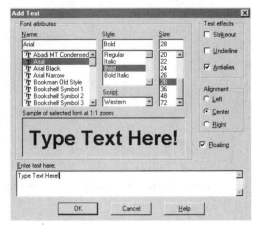

Figure 11.1 Paint Shop Pro's Add Text dialog box.

Figure 11.2 Zoomed image of type that is antialiased.

Figure 11.3 Zoomed image of type that is not antialiased.

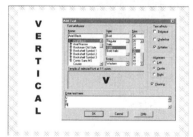

Figure 11.4 Setting down vertical type.

Figure 11.5 As shown here, text always remains highlighted until you officially place it down.

you may type, above the list, point sizes larger than 72.

6. Choose the effects you want to apply to the text, which include:

~~Strikeout~~

Underline

Antialias, which blurs and smooths the edges of the text

✔ Tip

■ When you want all your text to be one color (which is especially good when you plan to fill the text with other colors or patterns) do not choose Antialias. When you are sure that the color scheme of the text you want is correct, Antialias will give you much crisper-looking text. See **Figures 11.2** and **11.3**.

7. Finally, set your alignment, which includes three options: left, center, or right.

Alignment is useful only when you are trying to position multiple lines of text. It will then group them together and make the alignment go either left, center, or right.

✔ Tip

■ If you want to create a type effect as shown in **Figure 11.4**, just put a return after each letter and select center for the alignment.

8. After you have tweaked all the settings in the Text dialog box, you can click OK or just press Enter.

The words will appear on the screen as you specified. Text is not placed down until you click on the left or right mouse button. Until then, you can click on the text and move it to wherever you want on the page. See **Figure 11.5**.

Text is always placed down on the currently chosen layer. Always be sure to first select the layer on which you want to place text.

✔ Tip

- If you place down your text and decide that wasn't the right idea, an immediate Ctrl-Z (or Undo) will set the text back to a moveable selection.

To recolor type:

1. Create your text as stated on the previous page, but be sure to make sure you have deselected Antialias. Place down your text.

2. Click on the Flood Fill tool.

   The control panel should appear. (If it doesn't, click on the icon toggle control palette.)

   Once the control panel appears, change the tool's control by clicking on a fill style. You can choose what you would like to fill the text with, including a pattern, linear gradient, rectangular gradient and more.

   Click on the Options button to experiment using the preview box (see Figure 11.6). Then you can match that mode with either an RGB color, hue, brightness, or none.

   The Options feature lets you change the fill style and choose a blend mode. To the left of and under the preview box are the vertical and horizontal adjust bars. Click on the control button and drag it until you get the desired look, or simply type in the desired percentages in the available boxes.

   Each of the fill styles has its own adjustment controls. All the bars are easy to figure out— just play with them until you get the desired effect. When you are finished click OK. See **Figure 11.7**.

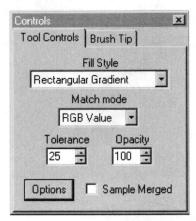

Figure 11.6 Set your options on the Fill palette.

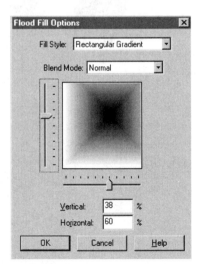

Figure 11.7 For this example we chose the rectangular gradient, which presents you with another dialog box allowing you to set specific gradient options.

Figure 11.8 The resulting recolored text.

Figure 11.9 Lay down your text and set your pattern fill.

Figure 11.10 Set your options on the Fill palette.

3. Once you have selected all of your options, the Flood Fill tool changes by adding a + symbol underneath the drip of the can. This means it is ready to fill your letters with the desired effects. Make sure the + symbol is inside the letter that is your target and click the left mouse button. See **Figure 11.8**.

There are two ways to create images like those shown in **Figures 11.9** and **11.10**. The first way is to use a standard image fill.

To use an image to fill text:

1. Open a new image on the screen. Then open an existing image which will be the image used to fill your text. Choose the Flood Fill tool and open its control panel.

2. In the Fill tool control panel, set the fill style to Patterns and then click the Options button.

3. The responding dialog box lets you set pattern fill options. (For more on these features, see Chapter 7.) It is very important to choose the New Pattern Source. Click on the drop-down menu and choose from any of the images listed (note that in order to be selected, an image must be open in PSP). The picture box below will present a thumbnail of the image. After you decide on the blend mode (for a plain fill of the actual picture choose Normal), click OK.

4. Shift back to your text image. Make sure the Fill tool is on and click inside the letters. Part of the image will appear in each letter. Each letter will be filled with the imagery that exactly corresponds to the same position in the pattern source image.

✔ Tip

■ If you want to select a specific smaller area of an image as a pattern, do so by copying the selection to a new image and then selecting that as your new pattern source. Follow all the same steps to fill the text.

Filling text using pattern fill is a good way to create textured text. However, sometimes you want to simply drop down text "cookie cutter" style onto an area of an image. It's a shortcut way to create cool-looking text effects as seen in **Figure 11.11**.

To clip text onto an image:

1. Create a new image and load an existing background image.

2. Place down type without Antialias selected. White on black works perfectly.

3. Flip the background and foreground colors on the color palette.

4. Select and copy the text area as shown in **Figure 11.11**.

5. Switch the focus to the background image that you loaded in step 1 and choose to paste it as a transparent selection (Edit>Paste>Transparent selection or Shift-Ctrl-E).

6. You will be greeted with a floating selection which lets the background imagery shine through like a stencil. Position the image anywhere you like and when satisfied click the right mouse button to place it down. See **Figure 11.12**.

7. Crop the image to complete the design.

Shadow on text is a nice effect that can add some class to a heading. There are several ways to accomplish this task.

To create shadow type:

1. Start with a clean new image.

2. Since there are two types of shadows you can create, dark or light, decide which you want as this will affect the order in

Figure 11.11 Setting up for clipping text onto an image.

Figure 11.12 Clipping text onto an image is a fairly fast way to create pattern-filled text.

Figure 11.13 Using layers to create shadow type. Set down the darker type in the background or lower layer and then just position each layer as needed.

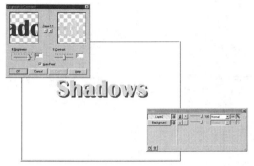

Figure 11.14 As shown here, when copying the text onto a new layer, you'll need to change the color of the text to create contrast, using an option such as the Brightness/Contrast dialog in Paint Shop Pro.

which you set down the type or arrange your layers later on.

3. Set down some type on a new layer.

4. Choose one of the following methods for creating shadow type that best suits your approach.

Via layers: Go to Layers on the tool bar and select duplicate. This will make a copy of the layer. Place this layer underneath your original text.

Lay down the same text but with a darker color (or if you've chosen a very dark color for your text, try a lighter color for contrast) on the new layer.

Select the Move tool and move the bottom layer text slightly to the right. By using layers you make it easier to adjust the shadow later. See **Figure 11.13**.

Via duplicating the text: This is a quick way to create a shadow effect—and you don't necessarily need multiple layers. After switching your foreground color to either a lighter or darker tone, click on the Type tool and render again the same text you just made. The Text tool saves the last type you created, so all you have to do is click OK.

Position the new text slightly askew from your original text. Although faster, this process is more permanent (you *may* be able to Undo your way back from a misstep) and doesn't provide the flexibility of a layered approach.

Via copying the text: While the text is still selected, copy the text (Ctrl-C or Edit>Copy). Then choose Paste As New Layer (Edit>Paste>As New Layer or Ctrl-L).

Select the secondary image and move it slightly. Change the color of this text by using any of the coloring options to lighten or darken either of the layers as needed. See **Figure 11.14**.

✔ Tip

- Blurring the shadow layer adds a stylish touch to a shadow type effect (see **Figure 11.15**). You can now blur the image by choosing the Blur filter (Image>Blur>Gaussian Blur) or any of the Blur choices listed in the Filters menu. You can also use the Drop Shadow Effect (Image>Effects>Drop Shadow) too (see **Figure 11.16**). For more on blurring filters, see Chapter 9.

Figure 11.15 The difference between adding a blur to the shadow layer (shown on the bottom) and not.

Paint Shop Pro has an automated process that is also useful for creating a drop shadow, giving a pleasing appearance to text (as seen in Figure 11.16).

To use Paint Shop Pro's automatic drop shadow:

1. Create the text—keep it selected.

2. Choose Feather from the selections menu (Selections>Modify>Feather or Ctrl-H) and set the amount to 4.

3. Go to the image drop down (Image>Effects >Drop Shadow).

4. A Drop Shadow box should appear.

5. Under attributes choose a color and then an opacity—remember: the higher the number, the darker the shade will appear.

6. Under Offset, choose vertical and horizontal—the higher the number, the more the shadow will displace out from under the type.

7. You can see what the shadow will look like in the preview box. Zoom in or out to see it better.

8. When you are all done making changes, click OK or hit Enter.

9. The image will now appear.

Figure 11.16 The results of running the drop shadow effect on the shadow layer of shadowed type.

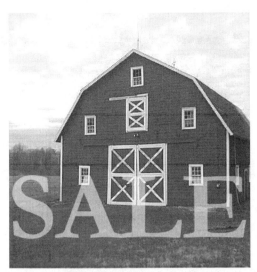

Figure 11.17 Screened-back type.

Figure 11.18 Type on a screened-back image.

Screen-back type makes the image show through the text as if you were looking through a screen to see it. This is really simple to do in Paint Shop Pro.

To screen back type:

1. Create three layers including a background layer.

2. Place your type in the topmost layer, your image in the middle layer, and a white background in the bottom layer.

3. To screen back the type, make sure your type color is white. Click on the opacity slider on the layer containing the type. Slide the dial to the left. Left will make the text fade into the background as seen in **Figure 11.17**.

4. To screen back the image, set the color of the type to black and slide the opacity down a bit. Then switch the middle layer containing the image and slide its opacity down below that of the type layer. The result of this can be see in **Figure 11.18**.

✔ Tip

■ Having a solid background, like white, helps to make the image clearer. If you don't have a solid background the black and white checkered back will show through. So, make sure the bottom-most layer is solidly filled in.

By using the Cutout tool in Paint Shop Pro we can easily create some cool 3-D type effects. The following steps show an example that creates 3-D style text. We chose to use some golden colors (which unfortunately can't be fully appreciated on black and white pages), but you can choose any fun combination of bright and light colors to create a similar effect. You can also do this on pattern-filled text (as shown later in **Figures 11.27** through **11.30**).

To use type and the Cutout tool:

1. Set foreground and background colors. The foreground color should be well contrasted with the background color. We set them to a golden hue.

   The foreground color was set to R:250 G:208 B:14 and the background color was set to R:193 G:161 B:13.

2. Set down some type and leave it selected until the entire process is complete.

3. Choose feather from the selection menu (Selections>Modify>Feather or Ctrl-H) and set the value to 3. See **Figure 11.19**.

4. Choose the Cutout tool from the menu (Image>Effects>Cutout). See **Figure 11.20**.

   ♦ Fill Interior should be unchecked.

   ♦ Shadow color should be set to Black.

   ♦ Opacity should be set to 100.

   ♦ Blur should be set to 14.

   ♦ The Vertical Offset should be set to −2.

   ♦ The Horizontal Offset should be set to −2.

   ♦ Once set hit OK or press Enter.

5. Choose the Cutout tool again from the menu. See **Figures 11.21** and **11.22**.

   ♦ Fill Interior should be checked.

   ♦ Interior color should be set to Foreground Color.

   ♦ Shadow Color should be set to Background Color.

   ♦ Opacity should be set to 100.

   ♦ Blur should be set to 7.

   ♦ The Vertical Offset should be set to 2.

   ♦ The Horizontal Offset should be set to 2.

   ♦ Once set hit OK or press Enter and remember to keep the text selected.

Figure 11.19 The type that works best is usually larger in size and not of the thin variety. This is 72-point Bookman Old Style. Note how the selection is feathered to allow room for the effects.

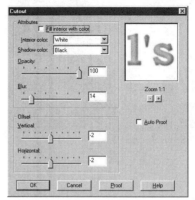

Figure 11.20 The Cutout dialog box as filled in for step 4.

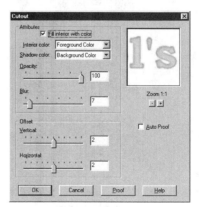

Figure 11.21 The Cutout dialog box as filled in for step 4.

Figure 11.22 A black and white representation of what the text should be looking like at this point in the process.

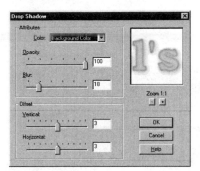

Figure 11.23 The Drop Shadow dialog box as filled in for step 4.

Fool's Gold

Figure 11.24 The final result; run the Despeckle filter if you notice small pixels of whiteness or darkness standing out.

6. Choose Drop Shadow from the menu (Image>Effects>Drop Shadow). See **Figure 11.23**.
   - ◆ Set the Opacity to 100%.
   - ◆ Set the Color to Background.
   - ◆ Set the Blur to 18.
   - ◆ The Vertical Offset should be set to 3.
   - ◆ The Horizontal Offset should set to 3.
   - ◆ Once set hit OK or press Enter.

7. Set the Foreground color to White.

8. Run the Hotwax Coating filter (Image>Other>Hot Wax Coating).

9. Run the Sharpen More filter (1-3 times), as desired (Image>Sharpen>Sharpen More). See **Figure 11.24**.

10. Optionally, run the Despeckle filter (Image>Noise>Despeckle).

✔ Tip

■ You are encouraged to play with all the settings in each step of the preceding process. Experimentation can lead to many derivative versions that either add a more intense 3-D look, or provide darker and lighter variants. In fact, a whole day spent repeating this process with different settings and recording the ones you like can give you a wide variety of possibilities. Type and the Cutout tool go together like peanut butter and jelly.

The Emboss filter can be run on type to create a simple 3-D effect quickly. The cool thing to do, however, is to create an embossing that can be transparently overlaid onto a picture.

TYPE AND THE CUTOUT TOOL

To transparently emboss type:

1. Load an image that you will use as the background.

2. Set the background color to the middle gray color (R:128 G:128 B:128) and the foreground color to black.

3. Place down some text and let it remain selected.

4. Expand the selection (Selections>Modify>Expand) by four pixels.

5. Run the Emboss Filter on the selection (Image>Other>Emboss).

6. Now you need to deselect the innards of each word. Carefully look for any selected area inside the text that is not black or white. Using the Ctrl key in conjunction with the Magic Wand, you can deselect these remaining areas.

7. Once you are satisfied that they've been deselected, copy the image (Edit>Copy or Ctrl-C).

8. Switch the focus to the background image and paste the image as a new layer (Edit>Paste>As New Layer or Ctrl-L). See **Figure 11.25**.

Adding texture to type is an easy way to make your text stand out. In the following case, we chose a brick texture we captured with our digital camera from a wall in our office. Photographic textures work the best for this.

To create "brick-styled" text:

1. Using a digital camera, take a close-up picture of a brick wall or any other interesting texture. See **Figure 11.26**.

2. Set your foreground and background colors to white.

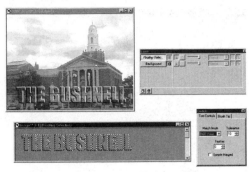

Figure 11.25 The Transparent Emboss effect in action.

Figure 11.26 Even a small texture will do, like this brick texture we captured with a digital camera.

Figure 11.27 Take the end product after step 9 and add a drop shadow (Image>Effects>Drop Shadow). The Drop Shadow box appears. Set the Color to Black, Opacity to 100, Blur to 5, Vertical Offset to 3 and the Horizontal Offset to 3. Click OK or Enter.

Figure 11.28 Take the end product after step 9 and use the Cutout tool (Image>Effects>Cutout). The Cutout box appears. Uncheck Fill interior with color. Set the Shadow Color to Black, Opacity to 100, Blur to 15, and both the Vertical and Horizontal Offsets to 3. Click OK or Enter. Run the Cutout tool once more. Uncheck Fill interior with color. Set the Shadow Color to White, Opacity to 100, Blur to 15, and both the Vertical and Horizontal Offsets to 2. Click OK or Enter.

Figure 11.29 This figure is derived from a combination of the effects in Figures 11.27 and 11.28. You can start with either one, but run through both the steps associated with Figures 11.27 and 11.28.

Figure 11.30 Take the image created in Figure 11.29 and then adjust the coloring a bit. Choose Adjust Brightness/Contrast from the Color menu (Color> Adjust>Brightness/Contrast or Shift-B). The Brightness/ Contrast box appears. Push up the Brightness (to 14) and the Contrast to further emphasize the effects of the Cutout tool.

3. Create a new file and make it as big as you need and ensure that the color scheme is set to 16.7 million colors (24 bit).

4. Open the image file containing your brick picture.

5. Click and focus on the new image you made.

6. Set down some type. Note that larger, "fatter" style typefaces work best.

   Here we used a 125-point Bolded Verdana font that was antialiased, with centering and floating selected.

7. Don't deselect the type — just place it where you want it on the page and then click the Flood Fill button.

8. Select Fill Style>Pattern from the Fill menu. Set Matchmode to RGB, Value Tolerance to 10, and Opacity to 100.

   Next, click Options and set the Blend Mode to Normal and the New pattern source to the name you previously saved the brick image as. Click OK or hit Enter when done.

9. Finally, take the Flood Fill tool and place the (+) sign in the middle of the letters and click in every letter. Remember not to deselect the type until it's completely finished. In order to apply the effects shown in **Figures 11.27** through **11.30**, your type must remain selected.

SAVING AND CONVERTING

Being able to save and convert images is crucial in design work. You should save your documents frequently, because whenever you make significant changes to your work, especially with large files, you run the risk of crashing your system—and no one wants to lose hours of labor.

Even aside from the issue of crashing, saving lets you more easily revert to previous versions of your work, and of course you can't transfer work onto disk, or transmit it via e-mail without first saving it.

Saving in Paint Shop Pro can also involve converting. When you want to change a file's format, you save it to a different format. Paint Shop Pro also has a very useful batch mode, which allows you to change numerous files all at once from one format to another.

In this chapter, we cover everything you need to know about file formats, saving, and converting imagery with Paint Shop Pro.

Saving Imagery

You can save an image in Paint Shop Pro in a few different ways. You can choose from several menu selections including Save, Save As, Save Copy As, and Batch Conversion (**Figure 12.1**). (Batch conversion is farther down the menu—not shown here.)

Save is the most basic option. When a file is finished, you can simply save it to the hard drive or to a disk. The Save command is also used when a file had been previously saved, you've made changes to the file, and now you want to re-save the file with the same name and format, including the new image changes.

If you want to change the name or format of a previously saved file, use Save As. This allows you to save a file with a new name, a new file format, and a new location if desired.

The Save Copy As command allows you to take an image that is already saved and make a copy of it, whether for backup purposes or to send it to someone else. This is also a good command to use to save versions of an image you're changing, in case you want to back-track to a previous version—remember, the Undo option can only go back so far.

Use the Batch Conversion method when you have many files that you want converted to the same file format. Batch conversion is useful, for example, if you want to take a disk full of TIF images and have them quickly converted to JPEGs for use on the Web.

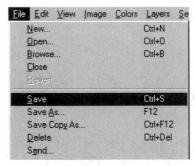

Figure 12.1 The basic menu choices for saving files in Paint Shop Pro.

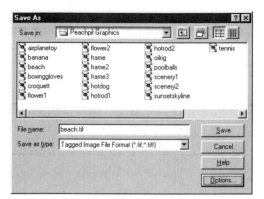

Figure 12.2 The basic Save As dialog box used to save files in Paint Shop Pro.

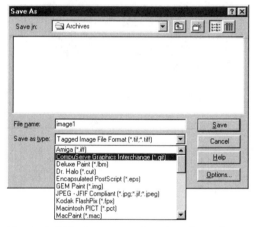

Figure 12.3 The Save as type drop-down list in the Save As dialog box makes it a snap to choose the file format for your image.

✔ Tip

- When saving a file, be sure that you don't type in a filename with an extension that doesn't match the extension associated with the file format you're using. This can interfere with the ability of Paint Shop Pro (and other programs) to load the graphic later on. Don't type extensions—always let Paint Shop Pro automatically set the extension.

To save an image:

1. Create an image or open an existing one.

2. Under the File menu select Save, or press Control-S, or use the Save button on the toolbar 🖫 that looks like a diskette.

3. If the image has not been saved before, the Save As dialog box appears (**Figure 12.2**). If the image has already been saved before, selecting one of the Save options will automatically save it to the previous location, under the previous filename.

4. If the image has not been saved before, you need to fill in a filename, select a destination directory/folder, and choose the format in which you want to save it. Paint Shop Pro uses the standard Windows Save As dialog box, which does not require much explanation—you should be familiar with saving files.

5. Select the directory/folder to which you would like to save the image. Make sure to select the appropriate drive. Once you select a folder, you will see all of the other images saved there that are of the selected format type (if any).

6. At the bottom of the dialog box is a drop-down list (**Figure 12.3**). Here is where you choose the file format for the image. To the right of that is a button marked Options. The Options button will present you with a specific dialog box that lets you set the options available for the specified file format, if it offers options. All these dialog boxes are covered separately at the end of this chapter.

7. When you have selected all the appropriate information, you can click on Save. This will save the image as the filename specified and in the correct directory.

To use Save As:

Using Save As is not much different from saving a file for the first time, as just described.

1. Start by creating an image or opening an existing one. Under the File menu select Save As (File>Save As, or F12).

2. The Save As dialog box appears (see Figure 12.2). The name of the file is the current filename, but you can change everything now, including filename, location, format, and format options.

3. When finished changing the setting, click Save. The file is then saved to its new location with its new name.

To use Save Copy As:

1. Open an existing image.

2. Under the File menu, select Save Copy As (File>Save Copy As).

3. The Save Copy As dialog box appears. This dialog box is the same as the Save As dialog box. The file can be saved with the same name because it is saved with "Copy" written after the name, once you click on Save in the dialog box.

4. When finished changing the setting, click Save. The file is then saved with the word "Copy" following the name of the file.

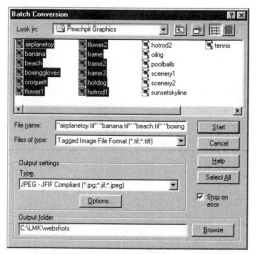

Figure 12.4 The Batch Conversion dialog box.

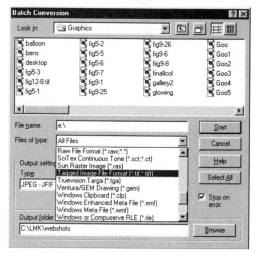

Figure 12.5 Choose the file type from a drop-down list to limit conversion to files of just those types.

✔ Tip

■ You can easily narrow the list of files to convert to a specific file type by selecting that file format from the Files of type drop-down list (**Figure 12.5**). Select that file type from the list. Paint Shop Pro will limit the files listed to only files in that format.

Batch Conversions

If all you want to do is convert a single file to another format in Paint Shop Pro, you can simply open the file and save it in a different format using the Save As command.

However, if you wanted to do that same operation over and over again, you should use Paint Shop Pro's Batch Conversion feature to perform a conversion on many files at once.

Note that although Batch Conversion can accept a plethora of files all in different file formats, it can only output all the new imagery into a single selected file format.

To use Batch Conversion:

1. Select Batch Conversion under the File menu. The Batch Conversion dialog box appears (**Figure 12.4**).

2. This dialog box looks a lot like the Save As dialog box, except it has additional options and features.

   The uses of some of the features in this dialog box are different from those in other dialog boxes. The Look In drop-down box shows the directory where the files to be changed are located. The drop-down menu will list all the available directories on your computer. Set this to the directory/folder where the files you want to convert are located.

   Once you have located the files, you can select them by clicking on them in the list of files below the Look In drop-down box.

3. To select a group of files, hold the Control key while clicking on files. The files you choose will be highlighted in the list. If the files you want are in a continuous column, hold the Shift key and click on the first file and the last file in the set. All of the files between and including these two selections will be highlighted in the list.

4. The files that have been selected for conversion are listed in the File name box.

5. Once you have selected all the files you wish to change, turn your attention to the Output settings features. Here you select the file type you desire, and where you want the files saved once they are converted. The Output settings allow you to select a file type in the Files of type drop-down box. This will be the new type.

6. Once you have selected a file type, click on the Options button. This allows you to select the options that are available for that particular file type (more on Options at the end of this chapter).

7. Once you've set the format, you must set the Output folder. Locate the directory in which to place all the new converted files. To select a directory, either type it in or click on the Browse button to the right of the Output folder box. Clicking on the Browse button will open the Browse for Folder dialog box where you can select a folder. Once you've done this, you will return to the Batch Conversion dialog box.

8. The Stop on error checkbox will stop the Batch Conversion if anything goes wrong with the program while the conversion is being done. If you want it to just keep going despite individual errors, leave this item unchecked. A log at the end of the process will show you any particular errors or problems you need to re-examine.

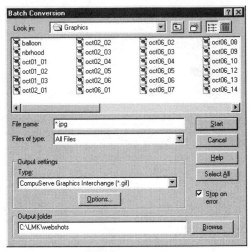

Figure 12.6 You can also type in one or more wild card filenames (such as *.jpg, *.gif) as a quick way to convert every file of a certain extension.

✔ Tip

■ If the files you want to change all have the same extension and exist in the same directory, you can just type in a wild card filename with the extension and automatically set up the conversion for all those files without having to select them. See **Figure 12.6**.

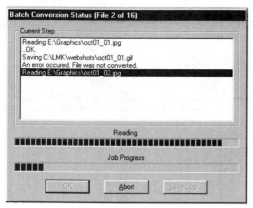

Figure 12.7 Once a conversion is underway, you can see a log of the events as they happen.

9. Once all the steps have been completed, we can begin the conversion process. To execute a batch conversion, you can choose between two options. One is to click on the Start button. This converts the specific files that you have selected, which are listed in the Filename box. The second is to click on the Select All button. This converts those images that contain the prefix that was entered in the Filename box.

10. Both of these options produce a Batch Conversion Status dialog box (**Figure 12.7**). This dialog box shows how long the conversion will take, and tells you at what point in the conversion process it is currently.

If you want to abruptly stop the conversion for some reason, there is an Abort button.

11. When the conversion is complete, click OK. A Save Log button becomes active. This log is a text list of all the processes done. If you chose to leave the Stop on checkbox unchecked when you started the conversion process, you can save this file and view it with a text editor to see if there were any errors in converting a particular file.

12. If you want to save the log, select Save Log to save the progress messages to a text file. If you don't need the log, just click OK to exit the conversion process altogether.

BATCH CONVERSIONS

Image Saving Options

Paint Shop Pro supports a large number of file formats. And many formats have specific options you can set that determine some of the additional characteristics of an image.

This section details the options that can be selected using the Options button in the save dialog boxes mentioned in this chapter.

It's important to know about the different formats and their options. Note that not every file type is listed here. If the file format doesn't have any particular options associated with it, we don't cover it. Paint Shop Pro's Help file also has additional background on the file formats it supports.

(CompuServe) Graphics Interchange Format

◆ **Format Extension:** .gif

◆ Developed by: Compuserve

◆ Background: Primary graphics format used on the Web for images with fewer than 256 colors. See **Figure 12.8**.

◆ Options: Choose one of two formats: Version 87a or 89a. Version 89a is the form most commonly used; it even supports animation. Version 87a older and doesn't support animation.

You may also choose between *interlaced* or *non-interlaced* format. When loading on the Web, interlaced formatting makes the graphic load every other line in the image until complete. This differs from the top-to-bottom load that is most often used. The result is that the user gets a rough idea of what the image looks like before the whole thing downloads.

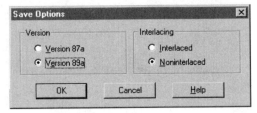

Figure 12.8 GIF image options.

Figure 12.9 JPEG – JFIF Compliant image options.

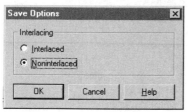

Figure 12.10 Portable Network Graphics image options.

JPEG - JFIF Compliant

◆ Format Extension: .jpg, .jif, or .jpeg

◆ Developed by: Joint Photographic Experts Group

◆ Background: Primary graphics format used on the Web for imagery containing more than 256 colors. Also used for large images that need lots of compression. See **Figure 12.9**.

◆ Options: There are two key options to consider. First, you may choose either standard encoding or *progressive*. When a Web browser loads a JPEG, if it is progressively encoded it will render the entire image over and over, so that it progressively goes from a blurry version to the final clear image. Standard encoding will display the image from top to bottom, but each line will be crystal clear.

The compression factor determines how small the format attempts to compress the image.

Portable Network Graphics

◆ Format Extension: .png

◆ Developed by: PNG Working Group

◆ Background: Created at first as a replacement for .GIF files when a patent issue cropped up. Offers more color support than GIF, too. Gaining ground as a native format supported on the Web (supported in Microsoft Internet Explorer 4.0b1 and later and in Netscape Navigator 4.04 and later). See **Figure 12.10**.

◆ Options: You can choose for imagery to be saved in an interlaced or non-interlaced manner (see .GIF for more explanation about interlaced vs. non-interlaced).

Kodak Flash Pix

- ◆ Format Extension: .fpx

- ◆ Developed by: Live Picture/Kodak

- ◆ Background: New graphics format for high-quality photos or photo-realistic images, becoming more popular for use on the Web (see Chapter 14 for more info). See **Figure 12.11**.

- ◆ Options: You can choose either a compressed or uncompressed file. If you choose to save it in the compressed format, you can set the amount of compression vs. image quality it uses.

Figure 12.11 Kodak Flash Pix image options.

Amiga

- ◆ Format Extension: .iff

- ◆ Developed by: Electronic Arts

- ◆ Background: Primary graphics format for imagery created and used on the Amiga computer platform. See **Figure 12.12**.

- ◆ Options: You can choose either a compressed or uncompressed file.

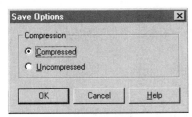

Figure 12.12 Amiga image options.

Deluxe Paint

- ◆ Format Extension: .lbm

- ◆ Developed by: Electronic Arts/Deluxe Paint

- ◆ Background: Primary graphics format used by imagery created by Deluxe Paint, a popular and out-of-print paint package created by Electronic Arts and used on the IBM. See **Figure 12.13**.

- ◆ Options: You can choose either a compressed or uncompressed file.

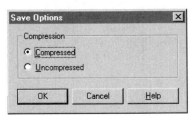

Figure 12.13 Deluxe Paint image options.

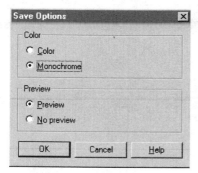

Figure 12.14 EPS image options.

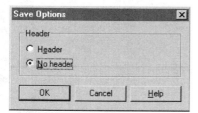

Figure 12.15 MacPaint image options.

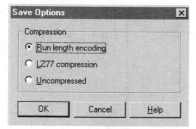

Figure 12.16 Paint Shop Pro image options.

Encapsulated PostScript

♦ Format Extension: .eps

♦ Developed by: Adobe

♦ Background: Primary graphics format for imagery that is rendered as a PostScript image. Used to send PostScript-formatted graphics over e-mail or on disk. See **Figure 12.14**.

♦ Options: You can choose for an image to be saved with color information or as a monochrome image. You may also choose whether it should save optional preview information, which can be useful for large files so users don't have to open up the entire file to know what the image looks like.

MacPaint

♦ Format Extension: .mac

♦ Developed by: Apple

♦ Background: Primary graphics format used by MacPaint, the original and still-popular graphics program for the Macintosh platform. See **Figure 12.15**.

♦ Options: You can choose to save the image with or without special header information about the image.

Paint Shop Pro Image

♦ Format Extension: .psp

♦ Developed by: JASC, Inc.

♦ Background: Primary graphics format used by Paint Shop Pro. See **Figure 12.16**.

♦ Options: You choose from three types of compression, Run Length Encoding, LZ77 Compression, or Uncompressed.

IMAGE SAVING OPTIONS

Portable Grayscale

◆ Format Extension: .pgm

◆ Background: Primarily used on Unix platforms. See **Figure 12.17**.

◆ Options: You can choose for it to be saved in ASCII or Binary format.

Portable Pixelmap

◆ Format Extension: .ppm

◆ Background: Primarily used on Unix platforms. See **Figure 12.18**.

◆ Options: You can choose for it to be saved in ASCII or Binary format.

Raw File Format

◆ Format Extension: .ppm

◆ Background: Lets you save the raw, unencoded RGB values of each pixel to a file in a variety of different ways. See **Figure 12.19**.

◆ Options: First, you may set a header of any number of bytes. Second, you can choose to have this header on the top or bottom of the image.

Once that is established, you may set how the RGB values for each pixel are stored in the file. You may choose to store them in planes, which will save three sheets of info, one each for Red, Green, and Blue information. You may also choose to save it in interleaved format with each line representing a single line of Red, Green, and Blue information.

Finally, you may set the order of the information to save either Red values first or the Blue values first.

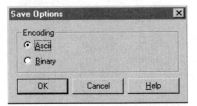

Figure 12.17 Portable Grayscale image options.

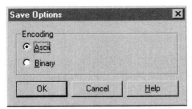

Figure 12.18 Portable Pixelmap image options.

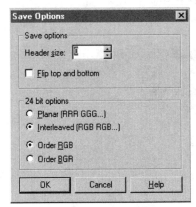

Figure 12.19 Raw File Format image options.

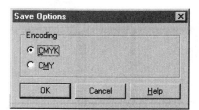

Figure 12.20 SciTex Continuous Tone image options.

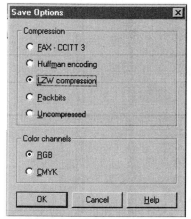

Figure 12.21 Tagged Image File Format image options.

Figure 12.22 True Vision Targa image options.

SciTex Continuous Tone

◆ Format Extension: .sct

◆ Developed by: SciTex

◆ Background: A CMYK format created by a high-end printing vendor. See **Figure 12.20**.

◆ Options: You can choose to encode the format for just CMY or CMYK.

Tagged Image File Format

◆ Format Extension: .tif, .tiff

◆ Developed by: Aldus Corporation (now part of Adobe)

◆ Background: Used quite a bit by graphic artists and popular for storing graphics in high-color format, without the loss of image quality that JPEG causes. See **Figure 12.21**.

◆ Options: You can choose one of several types of compression: Hoffman, FAX CCITT 3 (a TIF derivative used by popular Fax board software), Packbits, LZW, and uncompressed. You can then choose to store color information as either RGB or CMYK.

True Vision Targa

◆ Format Extension: .tga

◆ Developed by: Truevision

◆ Background: High-color graphics file format. See **Figure 12.22**.

◆ Options: You can choose the bit depth of the image (8- to 24-bit), and whether it is saved with compression or no compression.

IMAGE SAVING OPTIONS

Windows or CompuServe RLE

◆ Format Extension: .rle

◆ Background: Used by some Windows programs as an encoding method to store imagery. See **Figure 12.23**.

◆ Options: You can choose one of the two derivative formats of Run Length Encoding, Windows or CompuServe.

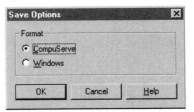

Figure 12.23 Windows or CompuServe RLE image.

Windows or OS/2 Bitmap

◆ Format Extension: .bmp

◆ Developed by: Microsoft

◆ Background: Major format for Windows raster imagery. Used as the format for storing Windows backgrounds and other Windows program imagery. Also used in OS/2. See **Figure 12.24**.

◆ Options: You can choose for it to be saved in Windows or OS/2 format, and whether the encoding is straight RGB or a run length encoding process (RLE).

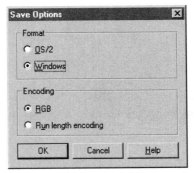

Figure 12.24 Windows or OS/2 Bitmap image.

Windows or OS/2 DIB

◆ Format Extension: .dib

◆ Developed by: Microsoft

◆ Background: Format used for Windows and OS/2 raster imagery. See **Figure 12.25**.

◆ Options: You can choose for it to be saved in Windows or OS/2 format, and whether the encoding is straight RGB or a run length encoding process (RLE).

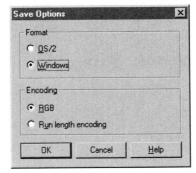

Figure 12.25 Windows or OS/2 DIB image.

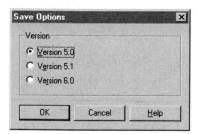

Figure 12.26 WordPerfect Bitmap.

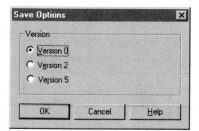

Figure 12.27 Zsoft Paintbrush.

WordPerfect Bitmap

- Format Extension: .bmp

- Developed by: WordPerfect

- Background: Used as the native graphics file format for WordPerfect. See **Figure 12.26**.

- Options: Choose the version number of WordPerfect with which it should be compatible: 5.0, 5.1, or 6.0.

Zsoft Paintbrush

- Format Extension: .pcx

- Developed by: Zsoft

- Background: Popular format in widespread use, associated with a painting program formerly marketed by Zsoft. See **Figure 12.27**.

- Options: You can choose the version of the format in which it should be saved: 0, 2, or 5.

PRINTING

Printing is an important part of graphics and design. If you are designing a logo that will appear on signs, letterhead, and business cards, you need to know that the image will print properly. If Grandma wants the Christmas pictures you took with your digital camera, and she doesn't have an e-mail account, you'll need to print out your images.

How to get the best output after all your hard work is what this chapter is about. Not only do we cover the basic options Paint Shop Pro offers you, but we also discuss the output options you have and add some tips about getting the best possible output.

Printing Options

Just as you now have a wide variety of scanners and image acquisition devices from which to choose (as discussed in Chapter 3), an equally diverse number of different printer types are on the market. In addition, you can choose to send your work to one of the many print shops that offer different levels of service—there's probably even a local Kinko's, Alphagraphics, or other copy shop nearby that can output graphics on a color laser printer for you.

It doesn't stop with printers either. Today you can find special types of paper for printing images, to enhance the presentation quality. You can print your image out on thermal transfer paper, and iron it onto T-shirts.

Let's walk through each available choice, and you will better understand which printer type best meets your needs.

Inkjet

The least expensive type of printer available for home use is an inkjet printer. They are usually 360 *dots per inch* (dpi) or fewer, so the image, which is good enough to put up on the refrigerator, is inadequate for professional work. If you just want to send a funny card you made to your Mom, inkjet is fine. Typically, you can print a couple of pages per minute.

Color inkjet

The next step up from there is a home color inkjet printer. Now you can send Mom a color card. A little bit more expensive than black and white inkjets, these printers are very popular today. Although the colors are usually less than perfect, the output is not bad.

✔ Tip

■ Home or small business color inkjet printers vary in quality, and the color output can differ a bit from what you get on the screen. Professionals offset this by using expensive color-correction tools, or by using higher-end printers and print shops. However don't just stand there and settle for sub-par output. When you have a color inkjet printer, print out some solid boxes of color: Red, Green, Blue, and some others like Yellow, Purple, and Orange. Compare these to your screen. If you notice the printer overcompensates with a certain tone, you can tone that color down in your graphic just before printing.

Laser

A real step up in the printer food chain is a laser printer. The most common types of laser printer are black and white models that print at 600 dpi. These can run from a basic home-use laser printer to a professional laser printer. Higher-end models offer greater speed and more memory to hold graphics and fonts for printing.

Color laser

Black and white printing has ruled the laser printer world for a long time. However, color laser printers are becoming more common. Color lasers image at the resolution of a laser printer, but with color. Low-end models can print at two to three color pages per minute. By using special paper, similar to that on which photos are printed, you can print out an image from your computer that looks very good.

Currently, most color lasers don't do a *terrific* job with color, although the technology is improving all the time. Older color lasers tend to produce a washed look in the colors, as opposed to ink jets which feature decent saturation as part of their printing process. To get optimal quality, use good quality paper and make sure the toner isn't running low.

Dye-sublimation

A cross between a laser printer and an inkjet printer, the dye-sublimation printer combines ink and heat to create high-quality color printouts. These printers are commonly used by service bureaus to preview imagery.

Dye-sub printers use ribbons coated with CMYK ink. Heat is applied to the ribbon, and the vapors from the ink are fused onto the paper. Unlike inkjet color, the results are better mixed and continuous in tone. These printers use specially coated papers to accept the heated ink and can be costly, but the results are very impressive.

Printing at copy shops

If no printer fits your bill (or budget), the best output can be found by going to a basic chain print shop like Kinko's or Alphagraphics. You can usually take your floppy disk to the shop and print it out using one of their computers. They have PCs and Macs, with an array of programs. Most have color laser printers available and will help you get a good printout.

Using a service bureau

A service bureau is more expensive than the local copy shop or Kinko's, but if you need great quality it is definitely worth it. Service bureaus give you more color options than most simple print shops, can print to film, and may offer a dye-sublimation printer or high-end inkjet. Your local yellow pages are a good resource for locating service bureaus in the area (look under graphic designers). There are also service bureaus on the Web (see **Figure 13.1**), which work via e-mail and overnight express.

Figure 13.1 Fayetteville, NC-based Digital Color Graphics is one of a number of Web service bureaus you can use.

✔ Tips

- Special paper can be purchased exclusively for use with inkjet and laser printers. When buying printer paper, make sure the paper is compatible with your specific printer, or else you can ruin your printer. There are heavy-stock papers that come in different colors for a professional look. Also, you can get heat-transfer paper especially for printers, so you can iron an image on a shirt or piece of clothing when you are finished.

- Some companies have created special printer paper that makes the image photo quality. The paper has the shiny gloss finish that makes it look like a true photograph. These can be used in laser printers or inkjets.

Photos

A final type of printer to look into is the *photo* printer. With the rise in popularity of digital cameras and photography, a number of major vendors are marketing these printers, which are designed to print out photo-quality images. They look better and have more continuous tones than images produced by a standard inkjet.

PRINTING OPTIONS

Printing in Paint Shop Pro

Printing in Paint Shop Pro is not a whole lot different than in most Windows programs. You have three main printing options in the File menu (see **Figure 13.2**): Page Setup, Print Preview, and Print.

Depending on the printer you own, different options are available to you when printing. These are usually found in the Printer Setup dialog box. Because every printer is different, we do not discuss every option for every printer.

We suggest you experiment with your Printer Setup. If this is your first experience with a graphics package, you will discover a number of options that might never before have seemed relevant.

That being said, let's run through the critical printer options and processes.

To use Page Setup:

1. Once you have an image and are ready to print, select Page Setup to tweak the printout. Under the File menu, choose Page Setup (File>Page Setup). The Page Setup dialog box appears (see **Figure 13.3**).

2. At the top of the dialog box is the Paper option. Choose a paper size in the Size drop-down box.

3. Next, choose how the paper will be fed into the printer in the Source drop-down box. There are usually only two choices: Paper Input Bin or Manual Feed. If your printer offers more choices, they will be listed here.

4. Choose Portrait (vertical) or Landscape (horizontal). An icon in the dialog box changes to show you a visual representation of the orientation.

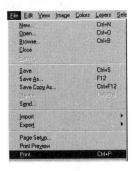

Figure 13.2 The Menu Choices for Printing.

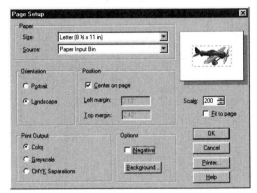

Figure 13.3 The Page Setup dialog box.

5. The Position option allows you to define how you want a printed image displayed on the page. The Center checkbox centers the image when checked. Left Margin and Top Margin let you decide how far from the left and top the image should be placed. The image in the top right changes to visually display the choice.

6. Print Output allows you to choose Color, Grayscale, or CMYK Separations for the image. If you have a black and white printer, you have nothing to worry about—it can only print black and white no matter what you choose. The image will come out the best using Color for a color image and Grayscale for a black and white image. CMYK Separations are used when you are taking your image to a professional print shop, which we discuss later in this chapter. CMYK printing generates four printouts, one for each color.

7. The Options section allows you to choose a Background color for the blank paper, or a Negative. Click on the Negative checkbox to force the printer to print out a negative color image. Like CMYK printouts, this is an option used by higher-end graphic and photography service bureaus. Most Paint Shop Pro users don't need it, but sometimes it just looks cool. Press the background button to bring up the Color Palette dialog to choose which color will be the background color for the negative image.

8. The Print dialog box also gives you a scaling option. This lets you take a very large image and print it at a fraction of its original size, or you can make a small image much larger than the original. By clicking on the Fit to Page checkbox, the image automatically enlarges to fit the entire page.

9. Once everything has been selected, click OK to close the dialog box and have all the options take effect. Or press Cancel to escape the dialog box and resume the original image settings

10. Clicking on Printer takes you to the Printer dialog box. We discuss this box later in the chapter, in the instructions on how to print.

To use Print Preview:

1. To preview an image before it is printed, select Print Preview under the File menu (File>Print Preview). The Print Preview window appears with the image set up on the page the way you selected in page setup (see **Figure 13.4**). The name of the image appears at the top of the box.

2. If you feel you image is perfectly set and ready to print, click on Print. This takes you to the Print dialog box.

3. On the other hand, if the image is not exactly the way you had intended, click on the Setup button. This takes you to the Setup dialog box and you can make all the necessary changes. When you exit the Setup dialog box, you return to the Print Preview window. This enables you to view the changes you just made.

4. If the image is not large enough for you to view, click on Zoom In. If the image is too big and you want to view it smaller, click Zoom Out.

5. To return to the image you were working on, click on Close, and the box closes, allowing you to view the original image.

When you are ready to see how your image looks on paper, it is time to print.

Figure 13.4 Print preview in action.

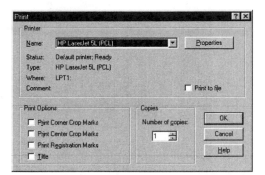

Figure 13.5 The Print dialog box.

To print an image:

1. Select Print under the File menu (File> Print or Control-P) or click on the Print button 🖨 on the toolbar. Once it is selected, the Print dialog box appears (see **Figure 13.5**).

2. The first option is the Printer. The type of printer you have installed should be listed in the drop-down box. There is also a list of all the other output devices attached to your computer, such as fax software. There should only be one or a few choices in the list, unless you have numerous printers attached to a network.

3. Status tells you if the printer is ready. Most printers say Default Printer, which is the printer that you probably set as your overall first choice. A Ready status indicates that the printer is online and able to accept print requests.

4. Type just reiterates the name of the printer you chose under Name.

5. Where refers to where the printer is located on your computer. It should say LPT1: if the printer is only attached to your computer. It will indicate a network location if you're on a network.

6. The Comment area displays information if the computer wants you to know something special about the printer; for the most part, this is left blank.

7. Across from the Comment area is a Print to File checkbox. When this box is checked, it prints the raw data to a file instead of to the printer itself. Print to File is usually used for higher-end graphics, and unless requested by a service bureau or printer, you will never need to use it.

8. The Print Options has four checkboxes. The first three deal with *crop marks* and the *registration*. Crop marks help identify where

the actual border of an image is. Registration marks are useful when lining up pieces of paper on top of each other; for example, when printing CMYK separation. Title prints the title that was put in the Image Information dialog box in the Creator Information section (see Chapter 2). If you did not fill in this section, it automatically prints the filename alongside the image.

9. The Copies option lets you designate how many copies you would like to print at once. Use the arrows to go up or down or fill the number in manually. If your printer does not allow multiple copies to be printed at once, the area is gray where the number would go. This option forces the printer to generate the extra copies, resulting in faster printing and less data going to the printer.

10. The Properties button takes you to the Properties dialog box. This dialog box allows you to arrange the settings for your specific printer. Due to the differences in printers, there is too much to explain here. You can consult your printer manual for further help.

11. Click OK to print the image — if the Print to File box is unchecked, a Status dialog box appears. If the Print to File Box is checked, the Print to File dialog box appears.

12. The Print to File dialog box asks you for a filename. The type of file is already set. It also asks for a folder. You can select the correct drive in the Drives drop-down menu. Click OK to print to the file.

Ten Things to Ask Your Service Bureau

Here are some things to ask when dealing with a service bureau or professional print shop.

1. The first and most important tip is to ask them what they need you to do to have the image *camera ready*. Camera ready means a final outputted image/printout that a printer will use for duplicating from.

2. Can they print color digital images directly from disk to paper or film?

3. In their color output systems, what is the highest dpi resolution supported?

4. What kinds of papers do they offer?

5. Can they print to film or does the image have to be printed on paper?

6. What are the compression schemes and file formats supported by their machines?

7. How can you send the work to them? Ask if they can receive the image through e-mail or if they need an FTP site.

8. If you have numerous photos or large files, ask if they have Zip drives.

9. If printing in color, find out what systems they use to output color digital images. Is it the quality you're looking for?

10. Ask how long the job will take, especially if time is a factor. Do not wait until the last minute to get things printed. Shops like Kinko's are open 24 hours, work fairly quickly, and can usually turn something around in a day or so, sometimes even in a couple of hours.

CREATING
WEB IMAGES

Paint Shop Pro is a great tool for creating
images for the Web. This chapter covers the
basics, including a discussion of the file formats you need to know to save your Web
imagery, as well as tips for making images,
such as buttons and backgrounds.

Basics of Web Graphics

Before we get started in this first of two chapters on Web graphics, let's go over some of the basics of creating graphics for Web sites.

Forms of graphics on the Web

Graphics on the Web can take many different forms, but they usually fall into two camps: imagery as shown in **Figure 14.1**, displayed for illustrative purposes (photos, charts, and artwork), and imagery displayed as part of the page interface (ad banners, backgrounds, buttons, rules, and image maps) as in **Figure 14.2**.

Overall, the goal of creating graphics for the Web is to make them both appealing and small in file size, two characteristics that can sometimes work in contradictory fashion. By maximizing the impact of imagery using fewer colors and by utilizing everything you will learn about the special file formats of the Web, you can easily create great imagery that won't take forever to load.

Screen size issues

Another important aspect of Web imagery is the size of the screens you expect users to view your pages with. There are three important dimensions to know about before you start creating your Web images.

The lowest and perhaps most common screen size is 640 x 480 pixels. Next is 800 x 600. And today, with better graphics cards and bigger monitors, many people are running their systems at 1024 x 768 resolution. Still higher resolutions like 1152 x 864 and 1280 x 1024 aren't as common—yet.

Screen size considerations are important because they dictate the height and width to your imagery must conform. No one likes to view images larger than their browser window (**Figure 14.3**). However, making an image too small can hurt your designs. Watch

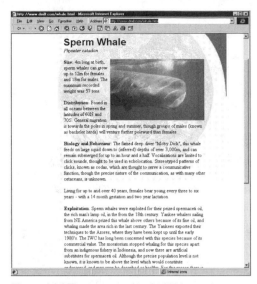

Figure 14.1 The image used in this Web page is obviously for an illustrative purpose.

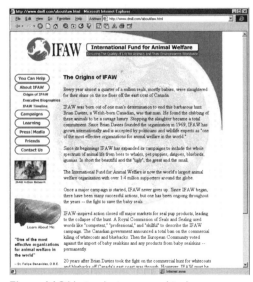

Figure 14.2 Notice the images used in the background, at the top, and the buttons alongside the text — all interface graphics created in Paint Shop Pro.

Figure 14.3 When you display an image bigger than the browser window scroll bars appear – avoid this.

how screen sizes affect some of your graphical design decisions.

File formats and optimization

The file format of your graphics determines not only size but also characteristics such as number of colors, how it loads, and whether it has a transparent background or is animated.

Several different formats and options are available for Web images. Each has unique characteristics you'll want at some point, and there are also ways to optimize under each format. The first thing you need to know is which situation to use each file format.

Optimization is important, your should try to create interface elements smaller than 20K without sacrificing appeal. At the same time imagery should look clean, and colorful while also not taking long to load.

From reducing color count and maintaining quality to choosing the right file format and options — look for every edge you can.

GIF

GIF stand for *Graphics Interchange Format*. The reason for saving graphics in GIF is to facilitate faster loading and take up less space.

GIF can only support 8-bit graphics (256 colors or fewer). Note that many computers are capable of 16-bit or 24-bit color. Use GIF to display simple graphics that don't require many colors. GIF makes a good choice for images with 256 or fewer colors. GIF is supported by all Web browsers.

To save an image as a GIF:

1. Create or open an image that you want to use on the Web.

2. Click on Save As or F12. The Save As dialog box opens. Choose the directory and folder.

3. Name your file in the File Name section. Then choose CompuServe Graphics Interchange (*.gif) as the Save As Type.

4. After you choose this file type, click on the Options button. The Save Options dialog box appears (**Figure 14.4**).

5. Choose Version 87a or 89a. Enable the Interlace feature by choosing Interlaced. The majority of GIFs on the Web are non-interlaced. (See the next section.)

Version 87a was the first version that CompuServe produced. Version 89a is the updated version released in 1989. The difference is that GIF 89a adds support for interlaced graphics and supports animation.

6. Choose all the options from the Save Options dialog box and then click OK.

7. Click Save. The image is saved as a GIF, and can be used on a Web site.

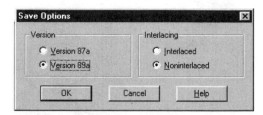

Figure 14.4 The GIF file format options.

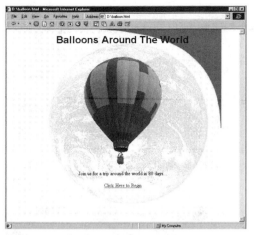

Figure 14.5 Notice how the balloon image has a transparent background letting the globe behind it shine through perfectly around its edges.

Interlacing and Transparency

The interlaced option is sometimes used to display graphics faster by showing parts of the image in intervals as it loads into view. Not many people use it, but you may find it suits your design. Interlacing works by saving the data in a way so that it shows every eighth row of the image on the screen first. Then it shows every fourth row, and every second row until the image is completely displayed.

To create an interlaced GIF:

1. To choose the interlaced option, simply follow steps 1 to 4 in the preceding section. When you get to step 5, choose your interlacing options.

2. Click on the Interlaced radio button.

3. Finish with the rest of the instructions on saving a GIF and then test your image in a browser to see the interlacing effect.

When creating a transparent GIF, the program allows you to make one color in the image transparent. The browser then does not display any information when it encounters the transparent pixels. Transparency is quite useful when you have an image that isn't rectangular in shape (see **Figure 14.5** for an example).

To create a transparent GIF:

1. Create a new image or open an existing one. Note that palette transparency only works with 256-color images, so if you load a high-color image reduce it first.

2. Click on the Eyedropper tool on the toolbar to pick the color you want to make transparent.

As you drag the Eyedropper over the image, the color in the box on the right-hand side of the screen changes according to whatever color the Eyedropper is currently over.

When the color you want to be transparent shows up in the box, click with the right mouse button.

3. Once you choose a color, select **Color** or Shift-Control-V).

✔ Tip

■ When the color is selected, a warning box may appear if the image has more than 256 colors. It will say you must be reduced to one background layer and 256 colors. You have to do this in order for transparency to take hold.

4. The Set Palette Transparency dialog box appears (**Figure 14.6**).

5. The choices available are No Transparency, Set transparency value to the current background color, or Set transparency value to palette entry and the number, which can be set using the spinner or entered by hand.

The No Transparency option undoes any previous transparency selection. The last two options are ways you can select the transparent color. For this example, we want to choose to store the transparent color in the background color setting.

✔ Tips

■ To select a palette entry, choose **Color>Edit Palette** or Shift-P.

■ The Edit Palette dialog box appears (**Figure 14.7**), containing all 256 colors or fewer in the image. Each color is represented in its own box—there can be two almost identical or even identical colors if you create one yourself, but each box is separate.

■ By clicking on a box a number appears in the bottom left-hand side of the dialog box, next to Palette Index. This number is the number you must remember to use to

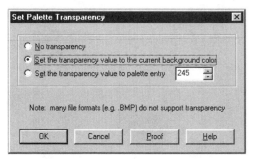

Figure 14.6 Palette Transparency Control dialog box.

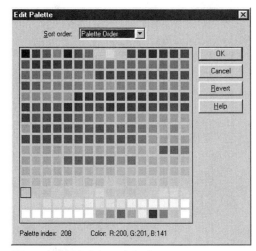

Figure 14.7 Edit Palette dialog box.

Figure 14.8 Proofing the transparency of your image. If the color disappears, you did it correctly.

set the transparency value to palette entry. This number must be entered in the box next to the Set the transparency value to palette entry command. After setting the number, you can go back to the Set Transparency dialog box and enter it.

6. To see what the transparency will look like, click the Proof button. This shows you how the image will look with the color you selected transparent (**Figure 14.8**).

✔ Tip

■ Sometimes when you click Proof you find that there are colors of the exact same hue or slightly varied that you want to be transparent but aren't. This is because although similar in color characteristics, they are actually pixels displaying colors that are in separate palette entries. You have to clean these up by hand by painting over those stray pixels with the paint brush set to the exact palette entry of the currently transparent color. This is why Proof is so useful—otherwise, you'd have to display it in a Web browser to make sure it was fixed.

7. When you have made a final decision about the transparent color, click OK. This removes the color from the image, and it can be now be used on the Web.

✔ Tip

■ Remember that only *one* color can be selected as a transparent color. If you go back and choose a new color as transparent, the old color that was selected as transparent will have its color returned to it. So, if you choose a color and decide that it is the wrong color, don't panic— just go back to the Set Transparency dialog box and change the settings.

Animated GIF

Animated GIFs are really series of images that, when put together, create an animation. To the viewer, an animated GIF is an image that changes slightly with each frame and looks like it is moving. By placing these images in order from start to finish and then running them, you can create animation similar to a flipbook. We discuss creating an animated GIF in Chapter 15.

JPEG

JPEG stands for *Joint Photographic Experts Group* and was created by that consortium of software developers who wanted a royalty-free file format that would look good, support millions of colors in a single image, and still compress well. JPEG compression means images may drop pixels and degrade in quality. However, depending on the image, you probably won't notice. JPEG is great for photographs and complex, colorful imagery but is not great for small resolution images, line drawings, or charts.

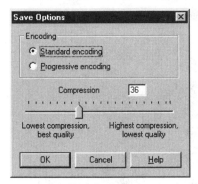

Figure 14.9 JPEG file format options.

To save a JPEG image for the Web:

1. Open an image and select **File>Save As**.

2. The Save As dialog box appears. Choose JPEG-JFIF Compliant (*.jpg, *.jif, *.jpeg), in the Save As Type drop-down box.

3. Once JPEG has been selected, click on the Options button. The Save Options dialog box appears (**Figure 14.9**).

   There are two levels of encoding in the JPEG format to choose from: Standard Encoding and Progressive Encoding, both of which are explained later.

   The other option is Compression amount. Use the Compression slider or fill a number in the box next to Compression. The numbers range from 1 to 99, from least compression to most. The lower the number, the larger the image file, and the better the quality.

4. When you finish setting options, click OK. The Save Options box closes and returns to the Save As dialog box.

5. After you select the appropriate folder, give the file a name, and choose Save As Type, click the Save button. The document is saved to the appropriate folder and is ready for the Web.

Standard and Progressive Encoding

Standard Encoding loads a JPEG image in standard format — that is, line by line, starting at the top and ending at the bottom. Progressive Encoding loads an image by displaying it first as blurry. As the image loads, it becomes sharper and clearer. By loading progressively, the viewer does not have to wait so long to get an idea of what an image looks like.

✔ Tip

■ Remember when you experiment to always give the image a new name so the original image is kept intact. This ensure that you always have the original to work from if there is ever a need to start from scratch.

JPEG

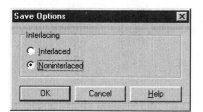

Figure 14.10 The PNG file format options dialog box.

PNG

PNG stands for *Portable Network Graphics* and was created when Unisys Corporation, which holds the patent on the LZW compression algorithm central to GIF, decided to enforce the patent they held on the compression scheme. Software developers, who had used GIF freely for many years, got together and designed a royalty-free format that offered many GIF features and then some. This became the PNG specification.

PNG is similar to GIF but does not contain LZW compression. Instead it uses more powerful compression that can handle 24-bit graphics that GIF cannot. Anyone can create PNG images and support them in their software free of charge because it is royalty-free. PNG supports interlaced and transparent images, just like GIF 89a. The disadvantage is that PNG is only supported in 4.0 browsers; older browsers require a plug-in.

To save an image as PNG:

1. Create an image or load an existing one.

2. Click **File>Save As**. The Save As dialog box appears.

3. Select a folder to save the image. Then select a filename and choose *.png from the Save As Type drop-down menu.

4. Click on the Options button. This opens the Save Options dialog box, where you can choose the interlacing type you want (**Figure 14.10**). Interlaced gives the same effects explained in the GIF Interlaced section. Non-interlaced loads normally.

5. Click OK when you finish the Options. You return to the Save As dialog box.

6. Click Save. The image is saved in PNG format and is ready for the Web.

PNG

FlashPix

Designed by Hewlett Packard, Microsoft, LivePicture, and Eastman Kodak, FlashPix is a royalty-free file format that is fairly new. It works a lot like JPEG. The compression scheme works the same as JPEG: with low compression, about 1 - 20, the image quality remains excellent, but the file size is large. Highly compressed, about 60-99, the file size is small, but the image quality suffers.

The benefit of saving an image as FlashPix is that the image is saved in three different resolutions: high, medium, and low. You can place the one file on your Web site, and from that the viewers can receive the resolution version that best suits their needs.

Note: Viewers need you to embed a certain Java applet on your site to view FlashPix. In the future, Web browsers may support FlashPix. For more on FlashPix and this applet, visit **www.livepicture.com** or **www.flashpix.com**.

To save an image as FlashPix:

1. Select Save As from the File menu. The Save As dialog box opens.

2. Select a folder in which to save the image, select a filename, and choose *.fpx from the Save As Type drop-down menu.

3. Click on the Options button. The Save Options dialog box appears (**Figure 14.11**). Choose the compression scheme for the image (1 is least compression, 99 is most).

4. Click OK when you have chosen the options. This returns you to the Save As dialog box. When everything is filled out properly, click OK. The image is then saved as a FlashPix image, and is ready for your Web site containing a Java applet.

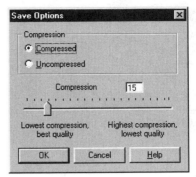

Figure 14.11 The Flashpix file format options dialog box.

FLASHPIX

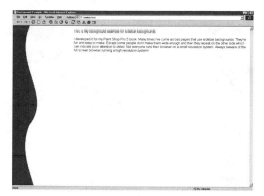

Figure 14.12 A properly constructed sidebar background should not tile in a maximized browser window.

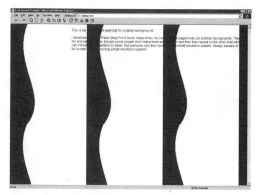

Figure 14.13 The result of an improperly constructed sidebar background.

Figure 14.14 The seamless background in this picture was created with a smaller sized graphic that tiled perfectly throughout the background.

Creating Basic Web Graphics

There are four major types of basic graphic elements you will encounter on the Web: Backgrounds, buttons, rules, and banners.

Backgrounds

Most people want their backgrounds to be perfect. However, when designing a background you don't intend to tile, be careful not to make it too small; otherwise, higher resolution systems with browsers running in a maximized state may cause it to tile, and the results can be disappointing.

Figures 14.12 and **14.13** illustrate this example. **Figure 14.12** shows a background capable of handling large and small screens. Our sidebar-style background looks fine and creates a clean look down the length of the browser window. **Figure 14.13** won't work for higher resolution because it was designed for a 640 x 480 screen—a mistake that shows through when a higher-resolution system brings up the page (as shown in the figure). Thus the challenge is double-edged: Design sharp backgrounds that don't get tripped up by higher-resolution users. One surefire way to avoid that problem is to create a "tileable" background that looks like one complete image as it seamlessly displays in a browser (**Figure 14.14**).

A sidebar background is a background image that is so long in size that it ends up tiling in a "stacked" manner. The result (**Figure 14.12**) is a background that creates a pattern running down one side of screen.

To create a sidebar background:

1. Start by determining how tall your background needs to be. The taller, the more memory it requires. **Figure 14.15** has a height of only 10 pixels. **Figure 14.16** stands more than 200 pixels high.

2. Set the height of the canvas as needed, but set its width to 1024 or higher. This gives you some assurance that you won't end up with it showing back up on the other side of the page if users with very high-resolution graphics view your site.

3. Draw your horizontal pattern. We recommend keeping it to 1/3 or less of the total length of the canvas on either side.

4. Make sure that the remaining area of the image is only one solid color, to minimize file size. Remember to make this color what you want the main background color to be. We chose white.

5. Save your image as a JPEG or GIF.

A seamless background is one that you intend to tile. (Don't end up with seams like those seen in **Figure 14.17**). Seams make you look clueless about creating Web graphics.

There are two tricks to creating seamless tiles. First, don't use imagery that doesn't tile well. This means choosing good patterns or abstract images that ultimately can blend well. Second, create a process that lets you identify seam problems and clean them up in the image.

✔ Tips

- For a quick but not-as-good-as-handmade out, use Paint Shop Pro's Create Seamless Pattern feature. This feature automatically turns any square or rectangular selection into a seamless tile. Choose **Selections> Create Seamless Pattern**.

- The best backgrounds are ones that present a good contrast with the foreground text. Mid-tone images will not work, and certain hues of very bright colors can be distracting. So as you make some early palette decisions, consider how contrast will affect the quality of your background.

Figure 14.15 A simple sidebar background: a long image 10 pixels high and 1152 pixels long.

Figure 14.16 A more complex background: a long image 200 pixels high by 1152 pixels long.

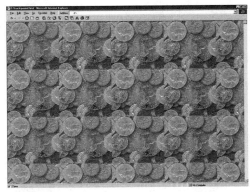

Figure 14.17 This background is not seamless and the result is ugly.

Figure 14.18

Figure 14.19 A tile rearranged so the seams show.

To create a seamless background:

1. Start a new document or select, cut, and paste from an existing piece of imagery.

2. When you are satisfied with your design or clipped image, increase the canvas size of the image (**Image>Canvas Size**) to three times the size of the tile or increase the canvas size of the current image. Position your image so you have space on the canvas to work (see **Figure 14.18**).

✔ Tip

- Now is the best time to reduce colors and size and generally optimize your tile to make it the best-looking, small-sized graphic you're willing to accept. Doing it after this step might jeopardize the seam removal process.

3. Select one half of the tile horizontally and cut it to the clipboard (Ctrl-X). Then paste it transparently (Ctrl Shift-E) back into the image. Position the selection on the other side of the tile.

4. Select one half of the existing tile vertically and cut it to the clipboard (Ctrl-X). Then paste it transparently (Ctrl Shift-E) back into the image. Position the selection on the other side of the tile.

   Now you should be able to see the seams the tile would produce. You've switched the sides to the outside and exposed the seams to the inside where you can cover them up. It should look like **Figure 14.19**. Four clear boxes separated by vertical and horizontal seams should be visible.

   You may be lucky and see very few seams. Otherwise, you need to remove these seams from the image to enable it to tile seamlessly.

5. To remove seams you have a few choices: Use the smudge tool (see Chapter 7) to move the graphics around within the

borders of the tile to produce a seamless image.

Use the cloning brush to remove seams.

Paint on new imagery or use the retouch tool with blur or soften to reduce the seam.

6. Once the seam is apparently gone, you're ready to use your background. **Figure 14.20** shows the tile with the seams removed. We painted over the seams with new rocks using the picture tube brush.

✔ Tip

■ Once the apparent seams are removed, you're all set. Note that depending on the specific imagery or pattern you've chosen to tile, it may not be possible to remove the seams. If it's not easy to remove them using smudge, soften, blur, or painting over it by hand, you're probably headed down the wrong path and should start over.

Figure 14.20 The final seamless tile.

Figure 14.21 A simple pattern button created using Buttonize.

Buttons

Buttons come in all shapes and sizes and can be created in various ways. For example, you can decide to make them all individual images or group them together into a single image and use an image map to separate each button on your page.

A button is usually a small graphic that may contain text denoting where it will lead you or what it will do when clicked. For example, a button labeled **HOME** would take a user to the site's home page. This section covers how to design several common styles of buttons using Paint Shop Pro. We leave it up to you to decide what sort of text or imagery you'll place on the buttons (our examples are primarily text.

To create a square or rectangular button from a pattern:

1. Load an image or create a pattern you'd like to buttonize.

2. Create a rectangular or square selection around it.

3. Choose **Image>Effects>Buttonize**. The Buttonize dialog box appears.

4. For the edge type, choose Transparent.

5. Use the Width and Height sliders to determine how large the button's edge should be. The opacity slider is used to determine how dark or light the edge should be. The higher the number, the darker the edges.

6. Click OK. The selection is now buttonized (**Figure 14.21**).

✔ Tip

■ If you need a smaller version of the button, reduce the image first before buttonizing.

We like solid-color buttons. Sometimes patterns can be a bit much and don't provide the crisp contrast that makes a button and its subject stand out.

To create a solid-color square or rectangular button:

1. Determine the button's background color by creating a selection (square or rectangle) and filling it in with the desired color.

2. Keep the selection active. Choose a different color for the edges. The best-looking buttons use a slightly lighter or darker color on the sides than on the face. Set your background color to the lighter or darker color, or any other color you prefer.

3. Once the background color has been chosen, you can create your button. Choose Image>Effects>Buttonize. The Buttonize dialog box appears.

4. Choose the Solid Edge option for the tile.

5. Use the Width and Height sliders to determine how large the three-dimensional edge of the button should be. The opacity slider is used to determine how dark or light the edge color should be (we typically set this between 70 - 100). The higher the number, the darker the color appears.

6. Once you have the correct settings for the button, click OK. The dialog box disappears and the selection is now buttonized (**Figure 14.22**).

✔ Tip

■ Sometimes an image made into a button looks better if you simply place a drop shadow behind it as seen in **Figure 14.23**. Choose Image>Effects>Drop Shadow. (For more on the Drop Shadow command, see Chapter 10.)

Why should all buttons be rectangular in shape just because the Buttonize command doesn't do anything else? With a little effort, you can create great-looking circular buttons.

Figure 14.22 Button created using buttonize on a simple filed rectangle.

Figure 14.23 A drop shadow effect adds a nice touch.

To create a circular button:

1. Create a new image. The New Image dialog box appears.

2. Choose 200 pixels for Width and Height. Leave resolution at 72 pixels per inch. Set the Background Color to White and choose 16.7 Million Colors (24-bit). Click OK. The new white canvas is created.

3. Click on the rectangular selection tool.

4. On the Tool Control, set the Selection Type to Circle, Feathering to 0, and place a check in the Antialias check box.

5. Drag the cursor over the image canvas. The plus sign on your cursor is the center of the circle. When you click and drag the cursor, the circle grows from both sides.

   Move the plus sign to the center of the page. Click with the primary mouse button, hold it, and drag to form a circle. Release the mouse button when the circle is an appropriate size.

6. Once the circle is formed in dotted lines on the page, click on the Fill tool.

7. On the Tool Control, set Fill Style to Solid Color, Match Mode to RGB Value, and Tolerance/Opacity to 100. Ignore Sample Merged because we only have one layer.

8. Click on the Options button. The Flood Fill Options dialog box appears. Make sure the Fill Style is Solid Color, and Blend Mode is Normal.

9. Click OK. You return to the Control Panel.

10. Choose a foreground color from the multicolor palette. Look for a color that isn't too extremely bright or dark; you want to be able to use contrast later to create a 3-D effect.

11. Choose a background color of the same hue, only darker, than your foreground choice.

BUTTONS

12. After you choose the color you want, place the cursor inside the selection and fill the circle.

13. With your circle in place, choose Image>Effects>Cutout.

14. In the Cutout dialog box (**Figure 14.24**), leave the Fill Interior with Color checkbox blank. Interior Color does not matter here. Set the Shadow Color to Background Color, so that the darker color appears.

Set Opacity to 100 and Blur to 0. For the Offset, set Vertical to −3 and Horizontal to −1. Click OK when finished.

Now that the dark side effect is complete, we need to have a light side. Go back to the multicolor palette and select a lighter version of your foreground color.

15. Run the Cutout effect again (Image>Effects>Cutout). Leave the Fill Interior with Color checkbox blank. Set Shadow Color to Foreground Color, Opacity to 100, and Blur to 0. Make Vertical offset +3 and set Horizontal offset to −1. Click OK when finished.

16. Now we have a good-looking three-dimensional circular button (**Figure 14.25**). Deselect the image unless you want to run other filters or effects on it. One good filter after the image is complete is the Blur or Blur More filter to blend it.

17. You can now place words on it or whatever you choose. In **Figure 14.26**, we simply wrote Click and added a drop shadow.

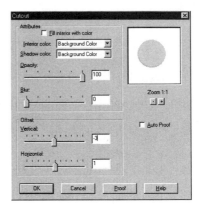

Figure 14.24 The Cutout dialog box with the settings for our circular button.

Figure 14.25 A nice, blank, circular button.

Figure 14.26 Our final product.

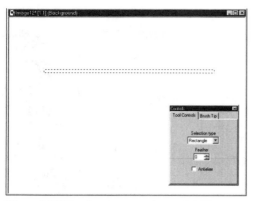

Figure 14.27 Just lay out your selection for filling in. Keep it narrow and between 400 - 600 pixels long.

Rules

Rules are used to divide sections of a Web page. Although you can easily place a plain rule using HTML's <HR> tag, some page authors like to create their own graphic rules.

To create a rule:

1. Create a new image. The New Image dialog box appears.

2. In the New Image dialog box, choose the Width and Height to fit the size you need for your Web site. Be careful not to create a rule much longer than 600 or you will create a rule that may outstrip the size of Web browsers running their screens or browser windows at 640 x 480.

3. Once you've created an new image canvas, start your rule by clicking on the rectangular selection tool on the toolbar. On the Tool Control tab, select Rectangle as the Selection Type, Feather to 0, and turn Antialias on.

4. Create a horizontal selection that is slightly higher and wider than the size of the rule you want to create as seen in **Figure 14.27**.

   You should now have a rectangular selection that is somewhat thin and almost as long as the page.

5. Fill the rule with an image or what ever color you would like.

✔ Tip

■ Gradients make great rules. Choose the Fill tool, and on the Fill control panel set the Fill Style to Linear Gradient, the Match Mode to RGB Value, and the Tolerance and Opacity to 100. There's no need for the Sample Merged. Click the Options button. The Options dialog box appears.

RULES

6. Choose the direction you want the gradient to form by moving the Direction dial or entering a degree in the Degree box. In our example (**Figure 14.28**), the degree is 338 and the Blend Mode is Normal.

Our fill style is what we chose on the Control Panel: Linear Gradient. When the degree is set, click OK. You will then be returned to the control panel and the canvas with the ruled selection on it.

7. Fill the selection with your gradient.

8. With the rule still selected, choose Image>Effects>Drop Shadow.

The Drop Shadow dialog box appears. Set Color to Black, Opacity to 100, Blur to 5. Then set Vertical offset to 3 and Horizontal offset to 1. Click OK, and the final product should look like **Figure 14.29**.

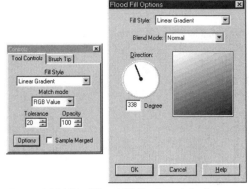

Figure 14.28 The Fill and Fill Gradient dialog boxes.

Figure 14.29 The final rule.

Where to Now?

At this point you should be familiar with the basics of Web image creation. However, there's much more to learn. If you've decided to stop here, make sure you eventually go on to the next chapter which discusses how to create image maps and animated GIFs and offers some general tips and tricks to optimize your imagery for display on the Web.

RULES

ADVANCED WEB GRAPHICS

In the previous chapter we covered the basics of Web graphics creation. By now you should be well on your way, creating buttons, backgrounds, rules and Web-formatted imagery. But wait, there's more! In this chapter, you will learn how to create some advanced Web graphics, and how to optimize your graphics for the Web.

More Web Imagery

There are three major types of Web imagery that have not yet been discussed. *Image maps* are images that contain hotspots on which users can click that link to other pages or content on the Web (more on that later in this chapter).

Animated GIFs are specialized versions of the GIF format that act like old-fashioned flip-books. They play back a number of images in rapid fashion to create animations. In Chapter 16, we discuss how to create an animated GIF using Animation Shop, the built-in animation editor that comes with Paint Shop Pro 5.0.

Banner ads are something we've all seen on the Web. These animated GIFs act as billboards on the information superhighway, announcing sales, new Web sites, and other advertising for surfers to see. When clicked on, they usually take you to the sponsoring organization's Web site. Most banner ads are nothing more than well-done animated GIFs. However, as we'll show you, there are some rules and regulations to which most banner ads conform.

One other possibility we'll explore is the use of graphical images to expand type options on the Web. We'll also show how the Web can display only a limited number of type styles; thus, many Web designers make use of type rendered as graphics to add some spice to their visual representations on the Web.

Figure 15.1 Using MapEdit32 to build an image map.

Image Maps

Creating an image map is a two-part process. This first part is creating the image in Paint Shop Pro. The second part is using an image map editor to create the HTML code used to make the map come alive.

To create an image map:

1. If you don't have a image map editing program, we recommend you download MapEdit 32 by Boutell.com, available at http://www.boutell.com/mapedit/.

2. As previously mentioned, image maps are nothing more than graphics with hyper-linked areas. Start developing one by loading or creating a graphical image you want to turn into an image map.

3. Save the graphic as GIF, JPEG, and PNG images. Then use it in an HTML file. MapEdit 32 does not load graphics directly; instead, you choose an HTML file to edit, and it then loads the graphics on that page.

✔ Tip

■ If you're not sure into which document you want to put your image map, create a simple HTML document containing just the image for which you're developing the image map. After creating your map, you can cut and paste the image map code into the HTML file in which you want to use it.

4. Load MapEdit 32 and choose **File>Open HTML Document**. Find the file and load it. MapEdit displays a list of graphics that the document references. Choose one from the list and it will load (**Figure 15.1**).

✔ Tip

■ Map Edit must be able to retrieve the graphic the HTML file references in order to edit it. Make sure that the graphic exists exactly where the HTML file says it does.

5. Once you've loaded the image file, a toolbar displays across the top of MapEdit (**Figure 15.2**). These are the tools you need to create various hotspot shapes for your image map. There is a square for creating rectangular hotspots, a circle for circular hotspots, and a triangle which lets you create polygonal hotspots.

6. To create a hotspot, choose a hotspot shape from the toolbar and draw it out on the image (**Figure 15.3**). For the rectangular and circular shapes, click once to start the shape, and then right-click to end it. For the polygonal shape, just click once with the right mouse button for each point, and then right-click to end the shape.

7. After you successfully create your shape, the Object URL dialog box displays (**Figure 15.4**). There are five textboxes you may fill in.

8. The only required field is the URL for clicks on this object. Type in the URL (Web address) to which this hotspot will lead the user.

9. The second field is alternate text, which displays if the image doesn't display on the user's browser.

   Target is used when you are using a framed layout and the URL is to be loaded into a specific frame. See an HTML reference for more information (we highly recommend *HTML 4 for the World Wide Web: Visual QuickStart Guide* by Liz Castro).

   The OnMouseOver and OnMouseOut are JavaScript references—consult a JavaScript reference for more information.

10. After you are done setting hotspots, save the file by choosing Save HTML Document from the File menu (**File>Save**

Figure 15.2 The MapEdit toolbar shows you the shapes you can use to define image hotspots.

Figure 15.3 A hotspot drawn in Mapedit32.

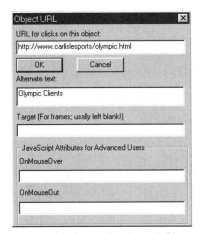

Figure 15.4 The MapEdit Object URL dialog box lets you type in the link information that is activated by an image map hotspot.

HTML Document). You can also use Save As to rename the HTML document something new. Also offered is Export Server Side map. This options outputs your image map file as a .map file, which can be used for server side image maps.

✔ Tip

■ MapEdit is shareware—if you use it a lot you should register the program.

Server Side vs. Client Side Image Maps

MapEdit lets you create server side and client side image maps. But what's the difference? Server side maps were the first to be used on the Web. Map files containing the coordinates and URLs for the image maps are stored on the server. A CGI program is referenced each time the user clicks on an image map. The program finds the image map file and loads the URL listed in the file. Server side maps are widely supported but are slower than client side. To use a server side map to support older browsers, consult with your Web hosting provider for the necessary CGI script.

Client side maps store the coordinates and URLs right in the HTML of the Web page. They work faster and don't tax the server as much as server side maps. Not every browser supports client side maps, although today most users are using browsers which do.

Banner Ads

Banner ads like those seen in **Figure 15.5** are the most popular form of advertising on the Internet. Although many advertising experts talk about moving "beyond the banner," it will be some time before that happens. Any advertiser on the Internet needs to be familiar with ad banner characteristics.

Once you know what, where, when, and how often to advertise, the next step is to create a banner ad. The first Internet ads were simple banners that sat frozen on a Web page, usually at the top and/or bottom. Animated GIF banners followed. As Web technology improved, the options multiplied. Ads can be animated GIFs, and can include drop-down lists, embedded search, and more.

To create a banner ad:

1. Set up a new document conforming to one of the standard banner sizes approved by CASIE (Coalition for Advertising Supported Information and Entertainment), as shown in **Table 15.1**.

2. If you are going to use Link Exchange (**www.linkexchange.com**), a popular, free banner advertising service (**Figure 15.6**), follow the rules in **Table 15.2**.

3. Create your banner imagery. If you want to create an animated banner, be sure to create all the key frames you need and save them as either separate files, or save each on a separate layer of a multilayer image. If you create a multiple layer file, be sure to save it as a PSP image.

4. If your image will be animated, use Animation Shop, the built-in animated GIF editor accompanying Paint Shop Pro 5.0 (see Chapter 16).

5. Make sure your resulting banner ad is less than 21K in size, unless otherwise

Figure 15.5 A typical banner ad is a long narrow graphic usually animated that when clicked on takes you to the advertiser's Web site.

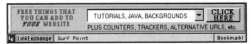

Figure 15.6 A typical Link Exchange banner has slightly different dimensions and rules than most other forms of banners.

Table 15.1

Standard banner sizes	
PIXEL SIZE	**BANNER TYPE**
468x60	Full banner (most common format)
392x72	Full banner with vertical navigation bar
234x60	Half banner
125x125	Square button
120x90	Button style 1
120x60	Button style 2
88x31	Micro button
120x240	Vertical banner

Table 15.2

Link Exchange banner rules
STANDARD BANNER
It must be in the GIF format.
It must be 468 pixels wide by 60 pixels high.
It cannot be larger than 10,240 bytes.
It cannot be animated.
It cannot be transparent (GIF Wizard will fix this).
The animation can last seven seconds.
It cannot loop (Link Exchange adds that itself).

indicated by a service or site on which you may be advertising.

✔ Tip

■ Use the browser safe palette on your banner ad for maximum optimization for the Web (see Browser Safe Palette later in this chapter for more details).

Text as Graphics

One of the simplest, but most effective, advanced Web graphics techniques is to use type rendered as graphics for your site, instead of relying on the limited number of fonts supported by most Web browsers.

On our site (**Figure 15.7**), we use some simple text rendered as graphics. This allows added flexibility in font size (we use the font Tahoma).

To render text as graphics:

1. Figure out the dimensions of the area your text will cover. Create a new image of that size and set it to 16 million colors.

2. Be sure to select the same background color as the one the text will be placed on. Using the hexadecimal codes in the color picker allows you to set the background to exactly match that of your site.

3. Using the Text tool (see Chapter 11), place your type down. Remember to use the antialias option. One of the compelling reasons for rendering text as graphics is that you can have smoother-looking text.

✔ Tip

■ Since your text is now a graphic, take advantage of cut and paste and kern letters and words together for best results.

4. In order to use antialias, your picture must be in high-color 16- or 24-bit mode. To lighten the load of the file size, reduce the number of colors down to 256.

5. Use the browser safe palette for optimal viewing possibilities.

6. Save the file as a GIF. Using JPEG may cause the text to appear imperfect, due to its compressed format.

Figure 15.7 Digitalmill's Web site is a good example of the text-as-graphics style of Web design.

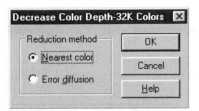

Figure 15.8 The color reduction dialog box for reducing from 16 million colors to either 64,000 or 32,000 colors.

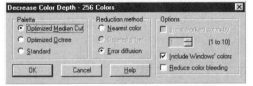

Figure 15.9 The color reduction dialog box for reducing from more than 256 colors to either 16 or 256 colors.

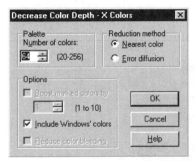

Figure 15.10 The color reduction dialog box for reducing the number of colors to between 20 and 256.

Optimizing Image Colors

There are several ways to approach the challenge of making your Web graphics both attractive and small in file size. First, you can limit the number of colors in an image; second, you can limit the size of an image; and, finally, you can try to compress an image file size.

File compression is covered in Chapter 14, where we discuss the different formats for Web graphics. Image size will be discussed later in this chapter. With regard to optimizing the color scheme, a basic rule applies: the fewer colors in an image, the better your chances of keeping the file size small.

To optimize color in an image:

There are four major dialog boxes associated with reducing the number of colors in Paint Shop Pro 5.0. See **Figures 15.8–15.11**. Each offers options tailored to the number of colors with which you are dealing.

1. The first dialog box, seen in **Figure 15.8**, is used when reducing from 16 million colors to either 64,000 or 32,000 colors. You are offered either the nearest color or error diffusion method of color reduction and nothing else (see the section "Color Reduction Methods" later in this chapter).

2. The second dialog box, seen in **Figure 15.9**, is used when reducing from more than 256 colors to either 16 or 256 colors. You may select a palette style, a reduction method, and utilize the boost colors option.

3. The third dialog box, seen in **Figure 15.10**, is used when you want to reduce the number of colors in an image to a specific number of colors between 20 and 256. You enter in that number, choose either error diffusion or nearest color, and designate whether or not you need to utilize the boost colors option.

4. The final dialog box, seen in **Figure 15.11**, is used when you want to reduce to only two colors (black and white). This offers some unique options.

First, you select the palette component to use. Often, the gray values option is the best, but you might want to select red, green, or blue if your image contains a great deal of one of those basic colors. For example, a shot of the sun setting might work best using the red component.

Next, you must select the palette weighting option. Choosing a weighted palette sets the image's current colors closer to black and white. This results in less dithering, less shading, and sharper edges. A non-weighted palette yields more dithering, more shading and softer edges.

Finally, you can select one of the three previously mentioned reduction methods. However, in this case, if you decide to go with error diffusion, you can choose from three additional sub-methods: Floyd-Steinberg (**Figure 15.12**), Burkes (**Figure 15.13**), and Stucki (**Figure 15.14**). Each is a different reduction algorithm offering a slightly different look. Experiment to find what you like best.

5. In each case, select OK when you are done, and the palette reduction takes place. Be sure to save your image first to avoid making an unwanted change. Although undo will most likely work, saving the image is the best method of protection.

✔ Tip

■ Before saving an image as a GIF image, do the color reduction yourself or suffer the consequences of an automated color reduction! Also, consider remapping the image to the browser safe palette.

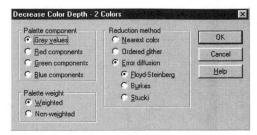

Figure 15.11 The color reduction dialog box for reducing to black and white.

Figure 15.12 Subtle as they may be, there are differences in appearance between Floyd-Steinberg…

Figure 15.13 Burkes…

Figure 15.14 And Stucki sub-method 2-color palette reductions.

Figure 15.15 Our original 16 million color image.

Figure 15.16 Nearest Color Diffusion many times creates blocks of colored areas increasingly as you reduce to less and less total colors.

Figure 15.17 Ordered Dither Diffusion many times results in an image which has areas of x-shapes, crosses, and grid-style patterns.

Color reduction methods

There are three major processes used to reduce the number of colors in an image, and one additional process using color commands.

You select a method by clicking on it in the Reduction Method group box. Depending on the number of colors with which you are working, you will be offered a choice of some or all of the following options (note that **Figure 15.15** is the original image):

Nearest Color method

No error diffusion is used. A total palette of the best 256 colors is created, and each pixel is evaluated to find the nearest matching color in the new palette. The pixel is then changed to that color. The resulting images have high contrast, but less gradation between different colors. **Figure 15.16** shows nearest color used on an image reduced to just 16 colors.

Ordered Dither method

Patterns of pixels are used to create a dithered reduction. Although it can work well for some images, most often this results in an image which has areas of x-shapes, crosses, and grid-style patterns. **Figure 15.17** shows ordered dither used on an image reduced to just 16 colors.

Error Diffusion method

This technique is used to reduce the number of colors in an image while maintaining color quality. The error diffusion method simulates colors by placing two different colors next to each other to create a third. For example, if you put a red pixel next to a white pixel, the area may look more like pink or light red to the naked eye. This reduces the number of colors, but your image may look a little more grainy. **Figure 15.18** shows error diffusion method on an image reduced to 16 colors.

Using the Reduce Color Bleeding option in error diffusion is highly recommended.

Palette options

When reducing an image to a palette of 256 colors or fewer, you can set some palette options: Optimized or the Windows palette. Within optimized, you can choose a median cut or optimized octree-style palette.

If you're trying to match up multiple images with the same palette, use the standard palette option; if not, select either one of the optimize options. Optimizing ignores the standard palette and develops a unique palette for the image that offers the best image quality.

✔ Tip

■ Sometimes you want to protect areas of an image from being affected by color reduction. When you reduce to a palette of 256 colors or fewer, you see an option in the reduction dialogs called Boost Mark Colors By. Check the box and enter a number 1-10 that allots palette entries to those colors. Those colors are protected during palette reduction. When selecting the Windows standard palette, boost colors is not an available option.

Figure 15.18 Error Diffusion most of the time is the best option for maintaining image quality—especially with photographic style imagery.

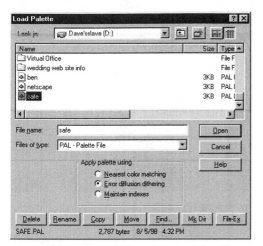

Figure 15.19 The Load Palette dialog box is just like a standard File Open box with the added options below the file window.

Using Browser Safe Palettes

One well-documented but often poorly understood issue concerning Web graphics is that of the "browser safe" palette. Lynda Weinman, a well-known author and graphic artist, has written extensively on this. Her books, *Coloring Web Graphics* and *Designing Web Graphics*, are excellent sources of information on using color on the Web.

What Lynda explains is that when you are designing graphics for optimal viewing by browsers with their screens set to 256 colors, as many older systems are, then using a browser safe palette on imagery is a necessary part of optimizing quality.

The browser safe palette is nothing more than a specialized palette of 216 colors which are shared by all the major browsers, for both Windows and Macintosh. The other 40 colors are reserved because either they don't match up, or they are used differently by each major browser. By removing them from the palette, you ensure that the image will be seen in the exact same manner by any browser.

To use the Color Safe palette:

1. Obtain a Paint Shop Pro 5.0-compliant color safe palette file. You'll find one at **www.dmill.com/safe.pal**.

2. Create your imagery and then reduce it down using the best color optimization process you can.

3. Load the new safe palette and remap the image. Choose **Colors>Load Palette** or Shift-O. The Load Palette dialog box appears (**Figure 15.19**).

4. Locate the directory in which you stored safe.pal, and then highlight it for loading. At the bottom of the file dialog are three options: Nearest Color Matching, Error

Diffusion Dithering, and Maintain Indexes. Choose Error Diffusion Dithering. Press Open when complete.

✔ Tip

■ Most of the time, Error Diffusion Dithering is the best method to choose. Choosing Nearest Color can work for very flat colored areas. Experiment to find the best choice under various conditions.

1. The palette will be remapped and the image displayed. Note that any changes to the image that may affect palette changes will break the safe palette.

2. Test the image in your browser. Switch your PC to 256 color mode if it's not there already, and look at the image. If the quality isn't good, try optimizing the image and reapplying the palette.

✔ Tip

■ Sometimes, when working in high-color 15-bit or 16-bit graphics mode with your PC, images saved with safe palettes can experience problems. If you don't think the safe palette is taking effect despite perfect execution, switch your PC to 256 color mode and repeat this process.

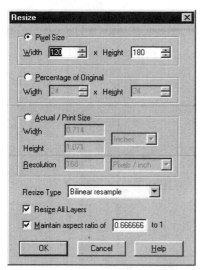

Figure 15.20 The Resize Image dialog box.

Optimizing Image Size

Here are the best ways to resize your images.

To resize an image:

1. Choose **Image>Resize Image**. The Resize Image dialog box appears (**Figure 15.20**).

2. This dialog box contains several ways to determine the resizing of the image. You can choose to resize by changing the pixel size, using a percentage or using exact dimensions. For Web imagery, the exact pixel size tends to be the best method.

3. At the bottom of the resize dialog are three options, which control additional aspects of the resizing.

   The resize method controls how the resizing is calculated. Choose the method that you think best suits the image.

4. The aspect ratio calculates how the revised dimensions are kept in proportion. As you enter one of the two items, height or width, the other is calculated to match the aspect ratio of the image. Leave this item checked to maintain aspect ratio.

   Uncheck this box if you want to create your own custom height and width; but be aware that the resulting image will most likely be disproportionately stretched.

5. The Resize All Layers checkbox lets you decide if you want to resize just the current layer or the entire image. Leave it checked to resize the total image.

6. After you have finished, click the OK button. The Resize dialog box closes, and the image (or layer) is resized.

✔ Tips

■ One important reason to resize imagery is to create thumbnails of large photographs. You can display a gallery of the thumbnails, which load more quickly, letting users click through to the larger-sized image.

- Some people, instead of creating a separate smaller version of an image, use the auto resize tags in browsers to merely shrink the larger image down. This, however, can cause it to take much longer to load the thumbnail page, since the Web browser has to load the larger image initially anyway. Always try to use quick-loading thumbnails for image galleries.

When resizing your image, you have four options, which determine how it goes about reducing your image size. These are useful to know about in order to make the best selection.

Pixel resize method

This method duplicates and removes pixels from the image as necessary to reduce the image size. Recommended for images featuring hard edges you want maintained. As seen in **Figure 15.21** this method isn't great for photographic quality imagery.

Smart size method

Paint Shop Pro chooses the best available method based on its internal analysis of the image data. Most of the time when reducing down this method choose Bilinear.

Bilinear

This method is only available for grayscale and 24-bit imagery.

The Bilinear Resampling method of resizing minimizes the raggedness normally associated with expanding an image, by using a process called interpolation. As applied here, interpolation smoothes out rough spots by estimating how the "missing" pixels should appear, and then fills them with the appropriate color. It produces better results than the Pixel Resize method with photo-realistic images and with images that are irregular or

Figure 15.21 Pixel Resizing doesn't work well on photographic quality imagery, but is good for images featuring hard edges like charts or graphs.

Figure 15.22 Bilinear resizing did a great job shrinking this balloon image in size.

complex. Use the Bilinear Resampling method for shrinking these images, and Bicubic for enlarging them. **Figure 15.22** shows an image we reduced using Bilinear resampling.

Bicubic

Best used for enlarging imagery only. Reduces the jaggedness associated with enlarging smaller imagery.

16

ANIMATION SHOP

With animated GIFs becoming an increasingly significant force on the Internet, the developers at JASC decided to build a specific tool for designing animated imagery. This program is Animation Shop, and it ships with Paint Shop Pro.

Although we can't cover every last detail of Animation Shop here, this chapter gives you all the information you need to develop quality animated GIFs from your Paint Shop Pro imagery.

Animation Shop Options

Animation Shop (see **Figure 16.1**) is a quick and easy way to create animated GIFs and banners for a Web site or presentation. The built-in animation wizard further aids you by making it very easy to quickly produce these animations.

Animation Shop works by letting the user create frames for the animation in Paint Shop Pro. These frames, shown in sequence from beginning to end, produce the animation.

When the individual frames are completed, the user opens up Animation Shop and loads all the frames in the proper sequence. Here you can choose many different animation effects, such as transitions between frames and text effects. These effects let you rapidly create simple animations without the need to create a complex animation on a frame-by-frame basis. Some of the choices are rotating or dissolving the image, or even causing it to explode!

To set Animation Shop's preferences:

1. To view or change the preferences for Animation Shop, select **File>Preferences**.

2. The Preferences dialog box appears.

3. To view the page that contains the information discussed below, click on the corresponding tab.

To set Frame View options:

1. Click on the Frame View tab on the Preferences dialog box. The options for the Frame View appear (**Figure 16.2**).

2. You can change the colors of the filmstrip border, the selected frames and the current selection. To change the selection colors, click on the Change button next to the corresponding selection. The color palette appears, allowing you to change the color.

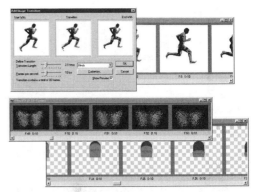

Figure 16.1 Animation Shop is a totally new product that ships with Paint Shop Pro 5.

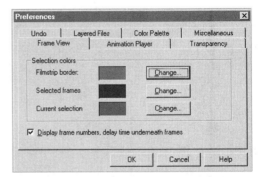

Figure 16.2 The Frame View preferences dialog box.

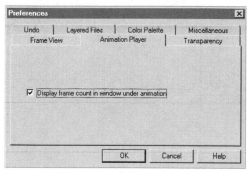

Figure 16.3 The Animation Player preferences dialog box.

3. The default color for the filmstrip border is gray. This will be the background color outside the frames section.

4. Next, you may change the color of the selected frame. The default color is blue. Thus, when you click on a particular frame, the border turns blue.

5. The last color change in this section is for the current selection. No matter how many frames are selected, this color denotes the last frame you clicked on. Therefore, don't make it the same color as selected frames.

6. The last choice you have on this page is whether or not you would like the frame numbers and delay time to be listed underneath the frames. If there is a checkmark in the box, these will be displayed; if you click on the box so that it is empty, these will not be displayed.

7. Click OK. Now you can return to your Animation Frame box.

To set Animation Player options:

1. Click on the Animation Player tab on the Preferences dialog box. The choices for the animation player is shown (**Figure 16.3**).

2. When you select View>Animation, the animation frames you have created are put together to show the animation.

On the bottom of this animation box, there is a number that corresponds with the frame being shown at each moment, along with a number denoting the total number of frames in the animation. For example, if the animation contains a total of 20 frames, and you are viewing frame number 12, under the image it would say **12 of 20**.

3. The checkbox in the Animation Player section allows you to decide whether or not you want those frame numbers to be shown when you play the animation.

If there is a check in the box, the numbers will be shown. If there is no check in the box, the numbers won't appear under the image while in the Animation Player.

4. Click OK. This closes the Preferences dialog box.

To set Transparency options:

1. Click on the Transparency tab on the Preferences dialog box. The Transparency options appear (**Figure 16.4**).

A transparency occurs when there is no background associated with an image. In these cases, a grid appears behind the image. The default is a white and gray grid in a checkerboard pattern.

In this section, you can change what the grid looks like. The Grid Size can be changed, using the drop-down menu, to a larger or smaller square size.

2. Change the color scheme using the Grid Color Scheme drop-down box.

3. When you choose one of the colors, the Color 1 box changes to the color selected in the drop-down menu, and the Color 2 box changes accordingly.

✔ Tip

■ The colors can also be changed by double-clicking on the Color 1 or 2 box. The Color palette appears, and you select the color.

4. All these changes can be viewed in the Preview box, which automatically changes when a new selection is made.

Remember: The grid sizes and colors are for your use only. When you place the animation on a Web site, the background will be transparent.

5. Click OK.

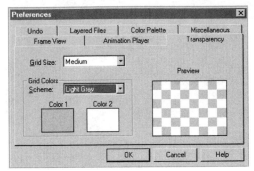

Figure 16.4 The Transparency options dialog box.

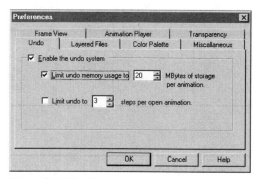

Figure 16.5 The Undo options dialog box.

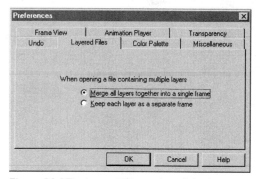

Figure 16.6 The Layered Files options dialog box.

To set Undo options:

1. Click on the Undo tab in the Preferences dialog box. The Undo options appear (**Figure 16.5**).

2. To use the Undo command, a checkmark must be present next to "Enable the undo system." This is the default setting.

3. Put a checkmark next to the command to limit the memory usage. Then you can use the spin control or type in a number.

4. The last option is to limit the Undo command to undo only a certain amount of steps per open animation. If this is checked, then you can limit how many steps you want to be allowed to undo. This saves disk space devoted to the Undo option.

5. Click OK.

If you create an image using layers, you must decide what to do with the layers once you load the image. Animation Shop does not use layers. You need to set Layered Files options.

To set Layered Files options:

1. Select the Layered Files tab on the Preferences dialog box. The Layered Files options dialog appears (**Figure 16.6**).

2. You can merge all layers into a single frame or keep each layer as a separate frame. Select one and click OK.

3. If you merge the layers together, there will be only one animation frame. If you choose not to merge them, each layer loads into Animation Shop as a separate frame.

✔ Tip

■ The "convert layers to frame" option allows you to use multilayered images in Paint Shop Pro to hand-draw animations. Just as traditional animators use multiple layers of translucent paper to draw animations, so can you with Paint Shop Pro. Simply use transparent layers and draw each new frame on a new layer, using the previous one as a reference.

4. When you decide how you want to open a file containing multiple layers, click OK.

To set Color Palette options:

1. Click on the Color Palette tab of the Preferences dialog box. The color options appear (**Figure 16.7**).

2. Checking the Use standard Windows color picker allows you to determine which color picker to use. If the checkbox is empty, you will use the color picker that comes with Paint Shop Pro 5.0. If checked, the standard Windows color picker is used.

3. Choose Decimal or Hexadecimal for color values. Default is Decimal. Hexadecimal is useful for coding in HTML. For most other uses, Decimal is fine.

4. Click OK when all choices are complete.

To set Miscellaneous options:

1. Click on the Miscellaneous tab on the Preferences dialog box. The Miscellaneous options dialog box appears (**Figure 16.8**).

2. You can specify whether the program should ask you if you want to save changes when you close a window.

3. If you do not want Paint Shop pro to ask you to empty the clipboard upon exit, click on the checkbox next to this option.

4. The splash screen is the information screen that appears when you first start the program. It indicates which version you have installed, who owns the copyrights to the program, and so on. If a checkmark appears in the box next to the image, the splash screen will display when the program opens.

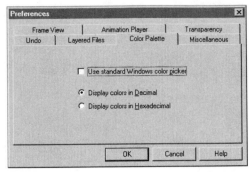

Figure 16.7 The Color Palette options dialog box.

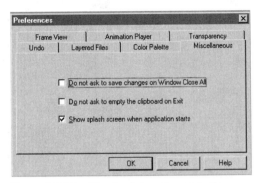

Figure 16.8 The Miscellaneous options dialog box.

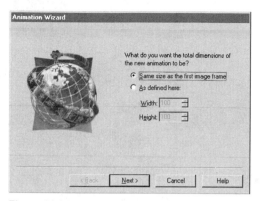

Figure 16.9 Define the dimensions of the new animation.

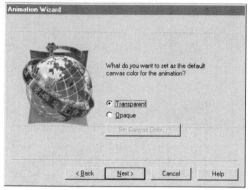

Figure 16.10 Set the default canvas color for your animation.

Animation Wizard

The Animation Wizard helps you through the process of creating an animation. It asks questions step by step. After you answer them all, your animation is complete.

To use the Animation Wizard:

1. Choose File>Animation Wizard.

2. In the first step (**Figure 16.9**), you are asked what the total dimension of the new animation should be.

   If you are loading images to put into the animation, it is wise to make all the frames the same size as the first image frame. The other option you have is to define the size of the frame here by choosing a width and a height in the appropriate boxes. When you have decided upon the dimensions, click Next. This takes you to the next set of questions.

3. The next choice (**Figure 16.10**) is the default canvas color for the animation. Transparent will have an empty canvas. When the image is on the screen, the background will be checkered. The Opaque setting will give the image a solid canvas in the color of your choice.

4. When Opaque is selected, set the Canvas Color. Click on the Set Canvas Color button, and the Color palette opens, allowing you to choose a color. When you decide on a color, click OK. This returns you to the Animation Wizard page. When you have made all the choices, click Next.

5. Where do you want the image to be located when it is loaded into the frame if it is not the same size as the frame? Your choices (**Figure 16.11**) are either the upper left-hand corner of the frame, or centered in the frame. If the image fills only part of the frame, you need to decide how you would like the rest of the frame

to be filled. Your choices for this are either with the canvas color, or with the contents of the preceding frame. Next, you need to scale the frames to fit. In this case, frames are scaled to fit the size of the overall animation.

When you have finished, click Next to move to the next question.

6. Now you may choose how often you want the animation to be repeated (**Figure 16.12**). You may click Yes, repeat the animation indefinitely, or you can choose to play the animation a certain number of times. You can select the exact number of times you want the animation to repeat.

   You can select how long you would like each frame to be displayed, in increments of 1/100th of a second. The default setting is 10. When you have made all of the selections, click Next.

7. The wizard (**Figure 16.13**) now lets you Add, Remove and Move the images into the order in which you want them. This is the last step in the Animation Wizard.

8. To Add images, click on the Add Image button. The Open dialog box appears, allowing you to select the images you want in the animation. For more on how to open an image, check out Chapter 2.

   You can select one image at a time, or select multiple images to load at once. If the images are all in a row, select the first image, then click and hold the Shift key. With the Shift key held, click on the last image to open.

   All of the images, in between and including these two images, are now selected.

9. When you have all of the images you want selected, click OK. The Open dialog box closes, and the images are placed in

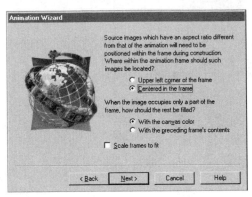

Figure 16.11 Where do you want the image to be located when it is loaded into the frame if it is not the same size as the frame?

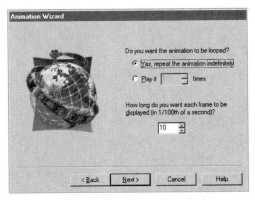

Figure 16.12 Choose how often you want the animation to be repeated.

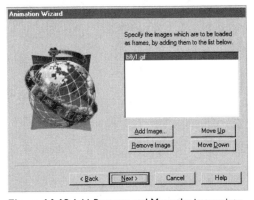

Figure 16.13 Add, Remove, and Move the images into the order in which you want them.

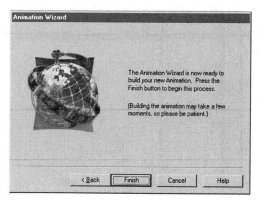

Figure 16.14 The screen indicates the Animation Wizard is ready to build your new animation.

no particular order in the white box above the buttons.

If you forgot to add an image, don't worry. Simply click on the Add Image dialog box and repeat the same steps.

10. If you added too many images, you can remove one by selecting the image in the white box above the buttons where the image is listed. The image is then highlighted, and all you have to do is click on Remove Image and the image is gone.

11. If the images are not in the order in which you would like them, you can move them up or down in the order. Select the image you want to move. If you want it to be moved up in order, click on the Move Up button. If you want it to be moved down, click on the Move Down button. You must click on either button one by one, until the image is in the appropriate position.

12. When all the images are in the appropriate position for the animation, click Next.

13. The screen will indicate that the Animation Wizard is ready to build the animation (**Figure 16.14**). Click the Finish button.

14. The result of all these steps is placed in order from start to finish on the Animation panel.

Image Transitions

Paint Shop Pro can help you automate the transition from one frame to the next, using Image Transitions (called *tweening* in traditional animation – filling in the minor frames between two key frames).

To create Image Transitions:

1. To add an image transition to an animation, select the first animation frame with which to work. Then select **Effects>Image Transition**. The Add Image Transition dialog box appears (**Figure 16.15**).

2. In the dialog box, there are three boxes. The image you selected is in the Start With box. The Middle box is the image displayed during the transition. The last box is the End With image. Not all transition types need an End With image, and the image disappears if it is not needed.

3. You can now Define the Transition and see how it will affect the image by looking at the Transition box.

4. Set the Transition Length in seconds using the Transition Length slider; this determines how long it will take for the image to go from start to finish.

5. The frames per section allows you to adjust how many seconds each frame is displayed. The dialog box tells you how many frames are contained within the transition you are viewing, not how many image frames you added to your animation frame.

   The difference is that by using the Image Transition option, the program is generating some of the frames necessary to create that particular transition from start to finish.

6. The drop-down box to the right of the dialog box contains all of the options you have for the transition. There are thirty transitions to choose from, from Blinds to

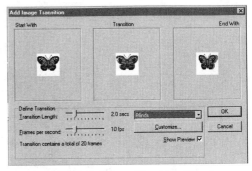

Figure 16.15 The Add Image Transition dialog box.

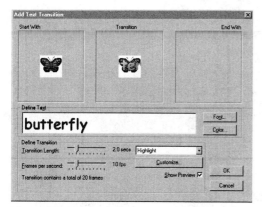

Figure 16.16 The Add Text Transition dialog box.

Zoom. There are too many options to describe each in detail here; try experimenting with each one to see what it does. With most of the options, you can click on the Customize button to customize that particular transition choice.

7. In order for the transition to show, you must have a checkmark in the checkbox next to Show Preview.

8. When you have selected all the desired options, click OK to accept the changes and generate the transition.

To create Text Transitions:

1. To create a transition using text, select the frame with which you would like the transition to start. Select **Effects>Text Transition**. The Add Text Transition dialog box appears (**Figure 16.16**).

2. You can type the text you want in the Define Text box. Once you have the text written, you can click on the Font button to the right of the dialog box.

3. The Add Text dialog box appears, and you can choose the font and size for your text, as well as type in text if you so desire.

4. Below the Font button is the Color button. Click on this button to select a color for the text. The Color dialog box appears to allow you to choose the color. For more on color selection, check out Chapter 2.

The other options are similar to the Image Transition dialog box discussed earlier. Different transition types are in the transition drop-down box. The Customize customizes some of the text transitions.

5. The Show Preview box must be checked in order to see an example of the transition.

6. Click OK to accept the changes and generate the Text Transition.

Editing Frames

With Animation Shop, can adjust each frame individually.

To edit individual frame characteristics:

1. Click on the frame you want to edit. Once the frame is selected, choose **Edit>Frame Properties**. The Frame Properties dialog box appears (**Figure 16.17**).

2. Click on the Display Time tab to set the display time for each individual frame. Whatever you set for the default will appear in the Display Time box. You can have a particular fram'e display for a longer or shorter amount of time. For example, perhaps you would like the middle frame to stay on the screen longer because it has some text on it.

3. Click on the Comments tab to type in comments to refer to later. The comments you type will not directly affect the program or the frame. It is useful to keep notes on why you did a certain thing to the frame, so you won't forget later.

4. When you have finished adjusting the comments, click OK.

To insert a frame:

1. You can add an additional frame to the animation, whether it be a blank frame or a picture frame. To do this, select **Edit>Insert Frames**.

2. When you select Insert Frames from the File menu, you will be prompted to choose either From Files or Empty.

3. Choosing a frame From Files inserts an image or picture frame. The Insert Frames From Files dialog box opens (**Figure 16.18**).

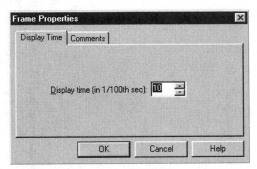

Figure 16.17 Set individual frame features with the Frame Properties dialog box.

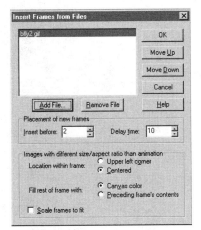

Figure 16.18 The Insert Frames From Files dialog box.

4. This dialog box is similar to the dialog box used in Animation Wizard. You may find some of the options are different, such as the Placement of new frames section. Here you can select where you would like the frames to be displayed. Use the spin control on the Insert Before box to choose the number of the frame before which you would like the new frame to be inserted.

You can choose a delay time in the box to the right of the Insert Before box. Just like the Animation Wizard, you can choose the location of the image in the frame.

5. When you are finished inserting frames, click OK.

6. If you chose **Edit>Empty from Insert Frame**, the Insert Empty Frames dialog box appears. In this dialog box, you can choose how many empty frames to insert as well as the location of the frame and its delay time. You can also choose the contents of the new frame. The choices are Blank to canvas color or Carry forward contents of preceding frame.

7. Click OK when all choices are made.

To delete a frame:

To delete an unwanted frame from the Animation Strip, simply select the frame you no longer want and then choose **Edit>Delete**. The frame is automatically deleted.

EDITING FRAMES

Animation Properties

You can control how an animation plays by editing Animation Properties.

To edit Animation Properties:

1. Select **Edit>Animation Properties**. The Animation Properties dialog box appears (**Figure 16.19**).

2. Click on the Looping tab; this allows you to change the options for the way in which the animation repeats itself. You can repeat the animation indefinitely or choose a set number of times to repeat using the spin control. Select one or the other.

3. Click OK when finished.

4. Click on the Comments tab to add the comments for the animation.

5. Click on the Canvas Color tab (**Figure 16.20**). Choose Transparent or Opaque. For Opaque, you can then click on the Set Canvas Color button to open the Color palette, where you can choose the color.

6. Click OK when all options are set.

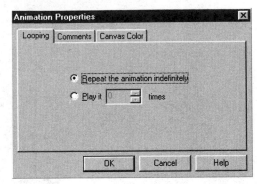

Figure 16.19 The Animation Properties dialog box.

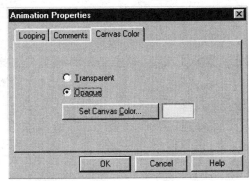

Figure 16.20 Click on the Canvas Color Tab to set the canvas color.

Figure 16.21 Testing an animation in Animation Shop.

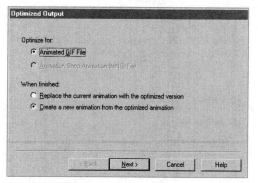

Figure 16.22 Animation Shop can easily help you optimize large animations for file size.

Testing, Optimizing, and Saving Animations

Where would animations be without testing, optimizing, and saving?

To test animations:

1. To see what the animation looks like before you use it, select View>Animation.

2. When a checkmark appears next to the word Animation in the menu, the animation is played from start to finish (Figure 16.21). To stop the animation select View> Animation again.

3. A smaller box appears, the size of a single animation frame, and the animation will run one frame at a time in sequence from start to finish. If you have told it to repeat, it will do so until you stop it.

To optimize animations:

1. To optimize the output of the animated image you just created, select File> Optimization Wizard.

2. In a fashion similar to the Animation Wizard, the Optimization Wizard asks you a series of questions. You make selections from the given options in order to complete the process and optimize the animation.

3. The Optimized Output dialog box appears (**Figure 16.22**) when you select File> Optimization Wizard. It will ask what you want to optimize for — either Animated GIF or the Animation Shop Animation (MNG), which can only be viewed in Animation Shop.

   Animated GIF is of course what you want if you're putting the animation on the Web. Next you will be asked whether you would like to replace the current animation with the optimized version or create a new animation from the optimized animation. If you think you might want to go back to the original image and make changes at some point, you should create a new animation from the optimized one.

4. Click Next to continue to the next page.

5. The Optimization Wizard gives you the opportunity to select the desired image quality for the animation (**Figure 16.23**). The higher the quality, the larger the animation's file size. The lower the image quality, the smaller the file size will be.

6. You can Customize the optimization settings used by clicking on the Customize button. This opens the Customize Optimization Settings (**Figures 16.24** and **16.25**), which lets you tell Animation Shop exactly how you want an optimized animation to be constructed when it optimizes an image.

   When you set the quality/optimization level, various combinations of these processes are used. However, you can now precisely set them here. Click Next to proceed to the next page.

7. The Optimization Wizard shows you that all of files are compressed (**Figure 16.26**) and prompts you to click Next to continue.

8. The Optimization Wizard shows you the results of the optimization (**Figure 16.27**).

9. Click the Finish button to complete the optimization process. If you wanted to create a new animation from this newly optimized one, the program creates it now.

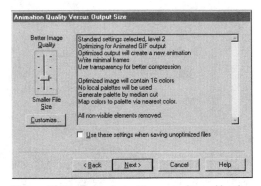

Figure 16.23 Set the desired image quality and let the Optimization Wizard do the hard work.

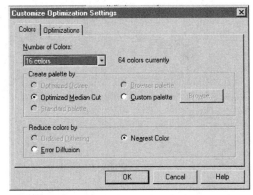

Figure 16.24 The first of two tabs which give you finite control over the processes used to optimize your animation.

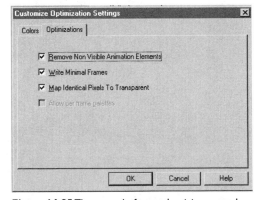

Figure 16.25 The second of two tabs giving control over the processes used to optimize your animation.

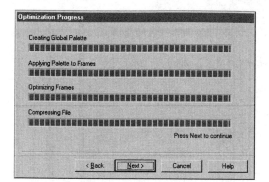

Figure 16.26 Animation Shop compresses the animation.

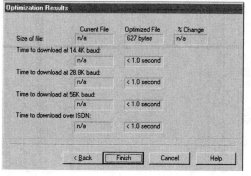

Figure 16.27 Your results give you an idea of whether you compressed it enough.

To save animations:

You save an animation the same way you would save any other image For more on saving, check out Chapter 12.

The only difference between saving in Paint Shop Pro or saving in Animation Shop is the Save as types.

1. In Animation Shop there are only two Save as types, CompuServe Graphics Interchange (.GIF) or Animation Shop Animation (.MNG). The GIF format is used to put the animation on Web sites and in programs other than Animation Shop, whereas the Animation Shop format can only be used with Animation Shop.

2. There are no options affiliated with these two Save as types.

3. Choose File>Save to save the image as either of the choices.

4. You can also save each frame individually by selecting File>Save Frame As.

WEB SITES AND RESOURCES

We hope we have answered many of your questions and provided a high-quality tutorial to Paint Shop Pro 5. For additional information, there are a number of Web sites where you can learn about the product.

Many of these sites offer interesting tips, tricks, and tutorials by people who have used earlier versions of Paint Shop Pro before moving to version 5. But most of their instructions work perfectly with version 5 as well.

All these sites are a testament to the wealth of information created by the community that has been built up by fans of Paint Shop Pro.

Tutorial Sites

APS Webgraphics

www.apmagic.au.com/graphics/graphics.html

Includes a number of tutorials and tips for Paint Shop Pro 5.

Free Web Graphics

www.dtp-aus.com/grafmain.htm

Includes a "How To" section that uses Paint Shop Pro as an example program for the various exercises, such as altering an image. A number of free images such as frames, round and square animated buttons, simple and 3D rectangular buttons, arrows, and assorted other graphics are here as well.

GrafoManiac

hem1.passagen.se/grafoman/

Another excellent resource, with tutorials, plug-in filters, and links to more resources. The creator of GrafoManiac runs the i/us Paint Shop Pro 5 area.

GrafX Design

www.grafx-design.com/Home.html

Offers tutorials for a number of products, including Paint Shop Pro. Tutorials include 3-D Buttons, Shadow Text, See-Through Text, Beveled Text, Embossed Text, and more. The site also includes product reviews.

i/us

i-us.com/

An outstanding resource for graphics creators, emphasizing Adobe Photoshop plug-in compatible products (such as Paint Shop Pro). The Paint Shop Pro Conference (i-us.com/paintshoppro.htm) is a live discussion board for users of the product. You can submit examples of your work for feedback and include details about your graphics and Web services to a free directory. Resources include discussion transcripts and industry news. There is a specific page called Chapter 5 that is dedicated to Paint Shop Pro 5 (c5.i-us.com), with tutorials, news, and links to other resources.

Jeff's Paint Shop Pro Tips

www.geocities.com/SoHo/2365/grab_bag_page.html

Features tips, related technical articles, links to other tutorial sites, and plug-in filter resources.

NightHawk's PSP5 Techniques

207.49.108.200/phase1/hawk1/

Includes techniques and links for Paint Shop Pro 5 users.

Paint Shop Pro Button Program Showcase

www.jasc.com/showcase.html

Jasc has developed its Paint Shop Pro Button Program Showcase to point Paint Shop Pro users to what the company considers outstanding Web work done using the program. There are several months' worth of selected sites. If you feel you have some work worthy of notice, submit your site using the submission form. If your site is selected, you will receive a complimentary Jasc title of your choice.

Paint Shop Pro Tips and Tricks

members.tripod.com/~jkhart/index.html

Includes a handful of tips on creating various effects such as neon glow, rough text, textures, hand-colored images, and so on. The site also includes links to a number of other Paint Shop Pro sites.

Paint Shop Pro Users Group

www.pspusersgroup.com

Offers tutorials, resources, reviews, news, and more for Paint Shop Pro users of all levels of expertise. The site also offers live chat sessions, an active message forum, a gallery in which members showcase their best Paint Shop Pro creations, and a tip of the week. Joining the Paint Shop Pro Users Group allows you to receive the Graphics Chronicle newsletter, discounts on software, and access to study sessions.

Sumrall Works, Inc.
Paint Shop Pro Resources

sumrallworks.com/freebies/buttonhole/psp/link2.htm

Includes plug-ins, Web tips, add-ins, art, tutorials, and links. The 5th Power section includes Paint Shop Pro 5 Tutorials.

3 Ring Circus

www.geocities.com/SoHo/7798/

Includes a number of tips for creating various graphical text effects.

Picture Tubes Sites

One of the most popular new features in Paint Shop Pro 5 is the Picture Tubes feature. Here are a few sites dedicated to Picture Tubes and their various uses. Most of these sites offer Picture Tubes available free of charge for non-commercial use.

Free Tubes

members.xoom.com/tubes/

Devoted to Picture Tubes and the art that can be created with them. The site includes more than 100 downloadable Tubes and clip art as well as Picture Tube tutorials.

JASC Tube Gallery

www.jasc.com/tubes/tubegal.html

Has a number of downloadable Picture Tubes, but you must first obtain the consent of the artist if you wish to distribute them or use them commercially. The page also includes instruction on how to add, edit, and create Picture Tubes.

Kathie's Web Graphics

www.cyberramp.net/~damddj/tubes.html

Includes a few downloadable Tubes and links to other Picture Tube sites.

Paint Shop Pro Tubes

babeard.simplenet.com/psp5.0_tubes.html

Features free Picture Tubes of animals, fish, insects, flowers, foliage, holiday-related items, and assorted other images. There are also links to other related sites.

Tube Garden

members.xoom.com/TubeGarden/tubes.html

The Tube Garden includes floral, nature, clip art, and miscellaneous Tubes as well as a handful of Tube links.

Free Graphics Resources

Jelane's Free Web Graphics

www.erinet.com/jelane/families/

An excellent, well-organized, and very useful collection of free Web graphics, including buttons, e-mail icons, and 256-color designs.

Xoom Software

www.xoom.com

Bullets, backgrounds, bars, icons, and much more, all free to use.

Amazing Free Stuff Pages

www.123go.com/drw/webs/graphic.htm

Covers all the best free stuff for Web people and has a very good — and up-to-date — list of some of the best free graphic sites on the Web.

KEYBOARD SHORTCUTS

Tool Palette Tools and Brushes

COMMAND	SHORTCUT
Zoom (Magnifier)	g
Deform	d
Crop	r
Mover	v
Selections	s
Freehand Selections	a
Magic Wand Selections	m
Eye Dropper	y
Paintbrush	b
Clone	n
Color Replacer	, (*comma*)
Retouch	z
Eraser	e
Picture Tube	. (*period*)
Airbrush	u
Flood Fill	f
Text	x
Line	i
Shape	l

File Menu

COMMAND	SHORTCUT
New	Control-N
Open	Control-O
Browse	Control-B
Save	Control-S
Save As	F12
Save Copy As	Control-F12
Delete	Control-Delete
Print	Control-P

Edit Menu

COMMAND	SHORTCUT
Undo	Control-Z
Undo History	Shift Control-Z
Cut	Control-X
Copy	Control-C
Copy Merged	Shift Control-C
Paste As New Image	Control-V
Paste As New Layer	Control-L
Paste As New Selection	Control-E
Paste As Transparent Selection	Shift Control-E
Paste Into Selection	Shift Control-L
Clear	Delete

View Menu

COMMAND	SHORTCUT
Full Screen Edit	Shift-A
Full Screen Preview	Shift Control-A
Normal Viewing	Control Alt-N
Image Information	Shift-I
Grid	Control Alt-G

Image Menu

COMMAND	SHORTCUT
Flip	Control-I
Mirror	Control-M
Rotate	Control-R
Resize	Shift-S
Crop to Selection	Shift-R

Color Menu

COMMAND	SHORTCUT
Brightness/Contrast	Shift-B
Gamma Correction	Shift-G
Highlight/Midtone/Shadow	Shift-M
Hue/Saturation/Luminence	Shift-H
Red/Green/Blue	Shift-U
Colorize	Shift-L
Posterize	Shift-Z
Edit Palette	Shift-P
Load Palette	Shift-O

Layer Menu

COMMAND	SHORTCUT
Select Active Layer	Control-(*Layer Number*)

Selection Menu

COMMAND	SHORTCUT
Select All	Control-A
Select None	Control-D
From Mask	Shift Control-S
Hide Selection Marquee	Shift Control-M
Inverse	Shift Control-I
Promote Layer	Shift Control-P
Float	Control-F
Defloat	Shift Control-F

Mask Menu

COMMAND	SHORTCUT
Hide All	Shift-Y
Invert	Shift-K
Edit	Control-K
View Mask	Control Alt-V

Capture Menu

COMMAND	SHORTCUT
Start	Shift-C

Window Menu

COMMAND	SHORTCUT
New Window	Shift-W
Duplicate	Shift-D
Fit to Window	Control-W

File Menu

COMMAND	SHORTCUT
New Folder	Control-B
Update Thumbnails	F5

View Menu

COMMAND	SHORTCUT
Refresh Tree	Control-F5

Find Menu

COMMAND	SHORTCUT
File Name	Alt-F3

Image File Menu

COMMAND	SHORTCUT
Delete	Control-Delete

Other

COMMAND	SHORTCUT
Center Floating Tool Palettes	Shift Control-T
Hide/Restore all floating palettes	Tab
Hide/Restore histogram	h
Hide/Restore layer dialog	l
Hide/Restore tool palette	t
Hide/Restore control palette	o
Hide/Restore brush dialog	b
Step through tools	Spacebar

INDEX

Italicized page numbers indicate references located in the appendix.

A

INDEX

X

Z

INDEX